Traditional Africa

Titles in the World History Series

Traditional Africa

by
Louise Minks

Lucent Books, P.O. Box 289011, San Diego, CA 92198-9011

Library of Congress Cataloging-in-Publication Data

Minks, Louise.
    Traditional Africa / by Louise Minks.
        p. cm.—(World history series)
    Includes bibliographical references and index.
    Summary: Examines the history and culture of Africa, from
ancient times through colonization and slavery to the twentieth
century.
    ISBN 1-56006-239-8 (alk. paper)
    1. Africa—History—Juvenile literature. [1. Africa—
History.]
I.Title. II. Series.
DT22.M55   1996
960—dc20   95-20851
                                                   CIP
                                                    AC

Contents

Foreword

Each year on the first day of school, nearly every history teacher faces the task of explaining why his or her students should study history. One logical answer to this question is that exploring what happened in our past explains how the things we often take for granted—our customs, ideas, and institutions—came to be. As statesman and historian Winston Churchill put it, "Every nation or group of nations has its own tale to tell. Knowledge of the trials and struggles is necessary to all who would comprehend the problems, perils, challenges, and opportunities which confront us today." Thus, a study of history puts modern ideas and institutions in perspective. For example, though the founders of the United States were talented and creative thinkers, they clearly did not invent the concept of democracy. Instead, they adapted some democratic ideas that had originated in ancient Greece and with which the Romans, the British, and others had experimented. An exploration of these cultures, then, reveals their very real connection to us through institutions that continue to shape our daily lives.

Another reason often given for studying history is the idea that lessons exist in the past from which contemporary societies can benefit and learn. This idea, although controversial, has always been an intriguing one for historians. Those that agree that society can benefit from the past often quote philosopher George Santayana's famous statement, "Those who cannot remember the past are condemned to repeat it." Historians who ascribe to Santayana's philosophy believe that, for example, studying the events that led up to the major world wars or other significant historical events would allow society to chart a different and more favorable course in the future.

Just as difficult as convincing students to realize the importance of studying history is the search for useful and interesting supplementary materials that present historical events in a context that can be easily understood. The volumes in Lucent Books' World History Series attempt to present a broad, balanced, and penetrating view of the march of history. Ancient Egypt's important wars and rulers, for example, are presented against the rich and colorful backdrop of Egyptian religious, social, and cultural developments. The series engages the reader by enhancing historical events with these cultural contexts. For example, in *Ancient Greece*, the text covers the role of women in that society. Slavery is discussed in *The Roman Empire*, as well as how slaves earned their freedom. The numerous and varied aspects of everyday life in these and other societies are explored in each volume of the series. Additionally, the series covers the major political, cultural, and philosophical ideas as the torch of civilization is passed from ancient Mesopotamia and Egypt, through Greece, Rome, Medieval Europe, and other world cultures, to the modern day.

The material in the series is formatted in a thorough, precise, and organized manner. Each volume offers the reader a comprehensive and clearly written overview of an important historical event or period. The topic under discussion is placed in a broad historical context. For example, *The Italian Renaissance* begins with a discussion of the High Middle Ages and the loss of central control that allowed certain Italian cities to develop artistically. The book ends by looking forward to the Reformation and interpreting the societal changes that grew out of the Renaissance. Thus, students are not only involved in an historical era, but also enveloped by the events leading up to that era and the events following it.

One important and unique feature in the World History Series is the primary and secondary source quotations that richly supplement each volume. These quotes are useful in a number of ways. First, they allow students access to sources they would not normally be exposed to because of the difficulty and obscurity of the original source. The quotations range from interesting anecdotes to farsighted cultural perspectives and are drawn from historical witnesses both past and present. Second, the quotes demonstrate how and where historians themselves derive their information on the past as they strive to reach a consensus on historical events. Lastly, all of the quotes are footnoted, familiarizing students with the citation process and allowing them to verify quotes and/or look up the original source if the quote piques their interest.

Finally, the books in the World History Series provide a detailed launching point for further research. Each book contains a bibliography specifically geared toward student research. A second, annotated bibliography introduces students to all the sources the author consulted when compiling the book. A chronology of important dates gives students an overview, at a glance, of the topic covered. Where applicable, a glossary of terms is included.

In short, the series is designed not only to acquaint readers with the basics of history, but also to make them aware that their lives are a part of an ongoing human saga. Perhaps they will then come to the same realization as famed historian Arnold Toynbee. In his monumental work, *A Study of History*, he wrote about becoming aware of history flowing through him in a mighty current, and of his own life "welling like a wave in the flow of this vast tide."

Important Dates in the History of Traditional Africa

B.C.

3.3 million
Small, near humans live in family groups in the Great Rift Valley in Ethiopia; similar, upright creatures leave footprints behind to be fossilized in volcanic ash in Laetoli, Tanzania.

2.4 million
The Stone Age begins; humanlike beings use simple stone tools in Olduvai Gorge in Tanzania's Great Rift Valley.

1.75 million
Humanlike beings live near Lake Turkana in northern Kenya.

250,000
Humans use well-shaped stone hand axes; they live nomadically in family groups.

6000–2000
Stone Age cultures flourish in the moderate climate of the West African Sahara region.

2000–1000
Dramatic climate change transforms West African Sahara region into a huge desert, causing African people to begin to move to other parts of Africa.

1000
Age of metals begins; Nok culture of Nigeria develops simple metalworking.

600
City of Meroë prospers on the upper Nile, dominating trade network between Mediterranean Sea cultures and inland Africa.

A.D.

300
Kingdom of Axum in Ethiopia conquers Meroë and controls trade network among Mediterranean, inland African, and Indian Ocean cultures.

450
Mediterranean contact brings Christianity to Axumite Empire.

700
Arab invaders conquer Axum; Muslim Arabs develop Zanj Empire and introduce Islam to Africa from Ethiopia down the coast of East Africa; Christian Ethiopians retreat to inland strongholds; Zanj Empire dominates Indian Ocean trade for seven hundred years; Ghana Empire rises along Niger River in inland West Africa, controlling camel caravan trade routes between Mediterranean and West Africa.

1000
Islam religion and culture spread to West Africa through caravan trade with Arab regions of the Mediterranean and Arab Muslim military campaigns in Africa.

1200
Sundiata, an African Muslim warrior, conquers Ghana, expanding it into larger inland empire of Mali; Ife culture prospers along the lower Niger River south of Mali.

1300
Zimbabwe culture in southeastern Africa establishes a trade network; in the Congo River basin most of today's Zaire is loosely governed by the combined Luba and Lunda kingdoms.

1444
European slave trade begins as Portuguese sail around hump of West Africa and develop trade relations with coastal cultures.

1450
Powerful Benin culture of Nigeria succeeds Ife.

1497
Portuguese mariner Vasco da Gama sails around the southern tip of Africa, opening Portuguese trade routes to East African coast, Indian Ocean, and Asia.

1500
Slaves become most valued African commodity purchased by Europeans for trade with colonies in North and South America; Arab traders on the east coast of Africa have well-developed, but lesser, slave trade to Middle Eastern and Asian countries; African kingdoms and societies at their height as European trade with Africa increases: merchant empire of Songhay, successor to Mali; Kanem-Bornu, a warrior-merchant empire near Lake Chad; Congo kingdom in Zaire; Zimbabwe kingdom; Zanj Empire of East Africa.

1505
Two-hundred-year struggle begins between Portuguese and the Muslim Arabs of Zanj Empire for control of East African coast.

1526
King Mbemba of Congo pleads with king of Portugal to end slave trade in his country.

1643
Queen Nzinga of Angola begins fight against Portuguese slave trade.

1652
Dutch establish first European settlement at Cape Town, South Africa.

1778
Society for the Abolition of the Slave Trade is established in England's North American colonies.

1788
As Europe's desire grows for raw materials to supply its new industries, the Africa Association begins sponsoring explorations of the African continent.

1800
Forty thousand African slaves a year are sold by European traders.

1832
British colonists move into South Africa; Dutch Boer farmers retreat inland.

1855
Slave trade is at its height in United States.

1857
Explorers Richard Burton and John Speke make first attempt to discover source of Nile River.

1865–1873
David Livingstone is sent by England's Royal Geographic Society to verify the source of the Nile; American journalist Henry Morton Stanley travels to Africa and in 1869 finds David Livingstone, who has been missing from world view for over three years; Livingstone dies in Africa in 1873.

1874
Stanley begins series of extensive explorations of African continent, particularly the Congo River basin.

1880
Much of Africa is claimed as colonies by European countries.

1884
Berlin Conference establishes rules for European claims on African territory.

1885
African resistance expands as Europeans rush to colonize unclaimed African territories.

1910
All of Africa is under European colonial control except for Ethiopia and Liberia, designated in 1847 as a homeland for freed North American slaves.

African Societies South of the Sahara

The traditional societies of Africa that developed south of the Sahara have received little attention in history books. When people think of Africa, they mostly think of Egypt, or Africa after colonization. People rarely think of the ancient kingdoms of Songhay, Benin, Zanj, and Zimbabwe.

Yet these ancient societies, and Africa itself, are important to the entire history of the human race. After all, the first hu-

Ancient African societies were isolated from other cultures until the 1400s. Once foreigners began exploring the continent, many of these traditional cultures were destroyed.

mans on earth lived on African soil. Later, while Greece and Rome developed sophisticated empires, in Africa great kingdoms flourished as well.

For the most part, the ancient African kingdoms south of the Sahara remained almost completely isolated from both their neighbors that bordered the Mediterranean Sea and from peoples on other continents. Uncharted oceans, enormous deserts, dense forests, and rushing rivers prevented foreigners and other African nations from trading with the largest part of the continent.

Foreign Interests

That isolation was abruptly broken in the 1400s, however, and Africa changed rapidly. Foreign ships began sailing around Africa, seeking to enter the interior in search of wealth. The most tangible form of this wealth were the African people themselves, who brought high prices in the slave market. Hundreds of years of slave trading contributed to the destruction of the rich African cultures that had been allowed to flourish deep in the interior for centuries.

Even after the slave trade ceased to be profitable, European countries kept their interests in Africa. These nations divided Africa among themselves, establishing colonies and seeking to eliminate the traditional cultures that they did not respect because they did not understand them. By 1900, every area of Africa except Ethiopia and Liberia was under European control, and the rich traditions and history of African cultures were smothered under colonial rule, and ultimately, their importance has been masked and ignored.

Yet this rich African history had a great impact on the development of West Africa, much as Greece and Rome influenced the development of Western Europe. African nations south of the Sahara developed sophisticated religious traditions and elaborate trade routes, built remarkable stone cities such as those in Zanj and Zimbabwe, and created early governments.

Africa played a critical role in the development of our human ancestors, and its early cultures remain a fascinating component in the entire history of human endeavor.

1 Birthplace of Humanity

Africa is the most important continent on earth for the study of the earliest humans. Most scientists now believe that Africa is the home of earth's first people. Many important discoveries of ancient human remains have been found in Africa, and each gives more information about early humans—where they lived, how they fed themselves, what tools they first used.

One day scientists Richard and Meave Leakey made a dramatic discovery near their work site at Koobi Fora. Koobi Fora is on the edge of Lake Turkana in northern Kenya, a country in East Africa about the size of Texas. This amazing find is only one of many that have occurred in the last fifty years in Africa.

> I was able to return to Lake Turkana for three months in the summer of 1969. . . . We had left our camels and temporary camp in the cool of the dawn and set out to walk among the fossil-beds, looking for interesting specimens. By 10 A.M., we had reached the furthest extent of the fossil deposits in that particular direction. My wife and I were thirsty, so we headed back in a more or less direct line to where we thought the camels were. While I was walking down a dry river bed, my eyes fell on something that made me stop

in my tracks: it appeared to be a hominid cranium [humanlike skull] sitting on the sand. We advanced to the spot to find the ancient bony face of an intact hominid skull staring at us. It was a truly extraordinary moment.[1]

Although estimated to be 1.75 million years old, the enormous jaw and molars of Nutcracker Man (bottom) are remarkably similar to the jaw of a modern Australian aborigine (top).

Scientists Louis and Mary Leakey use archeological tools while hunting for fossils in the Olduvai Gorge.

The skull proved to be that of a humanlike being dated at around 1.75 million years old. Nicknamed Nutcracker Man, he had large grinding molars for chewing. Now we know that humanlike beings lived in Africa much earlier than Nutcracker Man. In 1994 a remarkable discovery occurred in Ethiopia. Sixteen small, near-human individuals were uncovered who lived in East Africa over four million years ago. This is millions of years older than scientists thought possible just a few years ago.

An Engaging Mystery

The origin of humankind has been a mystery that every society has tried to explain. It is usually expressed in religious writings, oral traditions, and symbolism. Modern scientists and scholars also try to explain and understand this mystery. By using archaeology and the latest scientific dating methods, they test the age of ancient findings. The Leakey family of Kenya has been

immersed in this exploration for over sixty years.

In the 1940s Louis and Mary Leakey took their son, Richard, and his brothers on scientific expeditions. They often traveled into the extremely hot and barren Olduvai Gorge of Tanzania in East Africa. Mina Mulvey wrote about the Leakey family and their work in her young people's book, *Digging up Adam:*

Life at Olduvai was difficult. To avoid the worst of the heat, which sometimes reached 110 degrees Fahrenheit, they pitched their tent at the edge of the gorge, and each day, loaded down with digging equipment, scrambled down the steep slopes to the canyon below. . . . Day after day they toiled in the hot sun, first using picks and shovels to remove the overlying deposits of clay and sand, and then carefully probing the exposed site. Louis Leakey once described his fossil-hunting method. "It consists of crawling up and down the slopes of the gorge with eyes barely inches from the ground,

The First Man and Woman

"God looked at the earth, all black, without anything, and idle; he felt ashamed and wanted to do better. Nzame, Mebere, and Nkwa took counsel and they did as follows: over the black earth covered with coal they put a new layer of earth; a tree grew, grew bigger and bigger and when one of its seeds fell down, a new tree was born, when a leaf severed itself it grew and grew and began to walk. It was an animal, an elephant, a leopard, an antelope, a tortoise—all of them. When a leaf fell into the water it swam, it was a fish, a sardine, a crab, an oyster—all of them.

But Nzame, Mebere, and Nkwa took counsel again; they needed a chief to command all the animals. 'We shall make a man like Fam,' said Nzame, 'the same legs and arms, but we shall turn his head and he shall see death.'

This was the second man and the father of all. Nzame called him Sekume, but did not want to leave him alone, and said, 'Make yourself a woman from a tree.' Sekume made himself a woman and she walked and he called her Mbongwe. When Nzame made Sekume and Mbongwe he made them in two parts, an outer part called Gnoul, the body, and the other which lives in the body, called Nsissim."

stopping at the slightest fragment of a fossil bone or stone implement and delicately investigating the clue with a fine brush or a dental pick."

Using this painstaking technique, the Leakeys gradually uncovered an old land surface that had been occupied for hundreds of thousands of years. At Olduvai, humans had lived beside a lake and hunted the animals who came down to drink there. On this ancient living floor were hundreds of stone tools—pebble choppers, stone balls, waste flakes, what looked like crude attempts at hand axes, and vast numbers of bones of extinct animals.[2]

Scientists often do not have to dig through layers and layers of soil to discover human remains in Africa. Instead, portions of thigh, pelvic, or skull bones appear above ground. They are found in ancient rock shelters or along the worn banks of gorges and old lake beds. Each rainy season washes away more layers of soil, exposing fossil remains of plants, animals, and humans that are often millions of years old. The task of archaeologists is to identify sites likely to produce fossils. They must then patiently examine the area for clues leading to fragments of scattered fossils.

Archaeologists use careful methods for uncovering, preserving, and dating their finds. Once an area is targeted for research, it is mapped before anything is removed or uncovered. Grid lines are measured on the surface and marked with cord and stakes; then the location of every artifact found is recorded on a map. The map also indicates the layers of earth in which each item is discovered, a very important step for dating the artifacts.

The items removed from the site are dated through the latest scientific methods. Today's most accurate method is called potassium-argon dating, which works only with volcanic materials such as lava beds or volcanic ash. This method is particularly useful in Africa. Most of the African hominid finds have been in regions of intense volcanic activity such as the Great Rift Valley of East Africa.

Finding Lucy and the Footprints

While the Leakey family and their research teams are the best known of the scientists searching for human remains in Africa, many others are working toward the same goal. One of the most significant finds of all was made by Dr. Donald Johanson's team in Ethiopia in 1976.

Johanson focused on the Afar region of the Rift Valley in Ethiopia, where the valley broadens and merges with the Red Sea. In a spectacular discovery Johanson and his team stumbled on the remains of three-foot-tall Lucy. She was clearly an upright-walking human creature, yet she was two million years older than any other hominid found so far! About the same time, Mary Leakey uncovered an astonishing fossilized trail of human footprints in Tanzania. One set of footprints matched Lucy's foot structure perfectly, even though they were thousands of miles apart.

Dr. Donald Johanson displays a reconstruction of the skull of Lucy. Discovered in the Rift Valley of Ethiopia, Lucy is the oldest known hominid to walk upright.

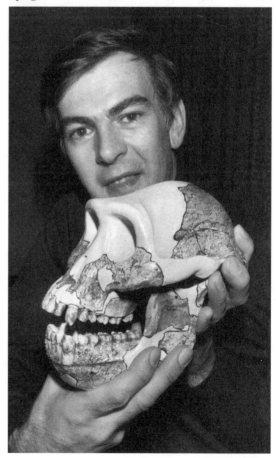

Although early humans were nomadic, they often returned to established settlements that were used as tool factories (pictured). In these factories, they created tools out of stone, wood, and bone.

Were Lucy and her human family the first type of human beings on earth? Discoveries are occurring so quickly now that ideas about human origins are refined each year.

How Did Early Humans Live?

The earliest humanlike creatures like Lucy and her family were nomads who followed the animal migrations. They gathered seeds, fruits, and nuts, and looked for water. They lived either in overhanging rock shelters in cliffs or in rounded houses made of skins stretched over bent poles. Some family groups began simple farming and stayed longer at a single site. Others returned again and again to settlements along rivers and lakes, using some of those sites as tool factories where they spent time creating their stone tools.

The first several million years in Africa are called the Stone Age because early people used only implements of wood, bone, and stone. Louis Leakey was intrigued by the rounded stone pebble tools and the shaped hand axes he found in the Rift Valley:

> Whenever he had a spare moment, he practiced making stone tools himself, using unworked lumps of lava or quartzite he found in the gorge and employing only those methods available to Stone Age man: dashing the stone that was to become a tool against a larger "anvil" stone. Or hold-

ing it steady and hitting it with another stone or with a piece of bone or wood, used as a hammer. In his first attempts he acquired more lumps and bruises than anything else. Later he became so expert that his productions could not be distinguished, except for the freshness of the worked surface, from those made by Stone Age man himself.

He also experimented with the ways in which these early tools must have been used. He once astonished onlookers by using a 25,000-year-old, two inch stone "knife" . . . to skin and cut up a gazelle. It took him only twenty minutes.[3]

Eventually the early human family groups in Africa collected into larger societies that developed villages, traditions, and a culture for the larger group. The earliest of these African cultures began in the interior of northern Africa in today's huge Sahara Desert.

The Fertile Sahara

On a modern map of Africa the most obvious land feature in northern Africa is the huge Sahara Desert. It stretches from the west coast to the east coast and is about the size of the United States. Millions of years ago the famous Sahara Desert did not exist. The region was a well-watered land with a flourishing culture.

Archaeologists have discovered that from 6000 to 2000 B.C. the Sahara was well populated. An advanced Stone Age society flourished and created magnificent rock paintings in Tassili in today's Algeria. The paintings record elegantly dressed women

riding tamed cattle, men with their herds of animals, and an abundance of wildlife. These people were probably the first farmers of Africa. An archaeologist described what the Sahara must have looked like in those early years:

> The plains were . . . covered with grass and populated with gazelle and antelope. What are now dry wadis [riverbeds] were rivers, fringed with dense bush or forest. Sediments and raised beaches show that swamps and lakes lay at the foot of many hills. They held Nile perch, crocodiles and

A prehistoric rock painting from Tassili depicts women, children, and cattle near a group of circular huts. Archeologists believe these early humans were Africa's first farmers.

A Stone Age Dinner

Layers in archaeological sites are labeled as soil beds. In this description from Maitland Edey's The Missing Link: The Emergence of Man, *the Leakey family notes interesting differences between beds.*

"Certain sites [in Olduvai Gorge] are rich in antelope bones, some with their skulls cracked open at the precise point on the front where the bone was thinnest. Others are crammed with the shells of large tortoises. One is littered with snail shells. Another contains a giraffe head, but nothing else belonging to that giraffe—clearly it was lugged in to be eaten at home.

A site higher up in Bed II reveals an increasing dependence on horses and zebras, which means that the climate had become drier by that time and was encouraging the spread of open grassland. There is also a marked increase of scrapers in Bed II, which suggests the beginning of an effort to work hides into leather."

hippopotamuses. Pollen samples indicate that the foothills were covered in . . . pine, cypress and juniper. The mixed oak woods of the upper slopes supported wild cattle and Barbarie sheep. . . . This rich ecological situation was very like the Nile valley.[4]

Then a dramatic climate change occurred around 2000 B.C. that forced the Sahara people to migrate to other parts of Africa. The weather became drier and hotter, gradually turning the fertile land into desert. Some of the people moved north toward the Mediterranean Sea, and some moved east toward the Nile River valley. Most of the people traveled south, primarily along the western coast of Africa and into the rich Congo River basin in the center of the continent.

Ever since that great migration out of the Sahara, African history has been divided by the presence of the Sahara Desert. Societies near the busy Mediterranean Sea were strongly influenced by ongoing contact with European and Middle Eastern cultures. The remainder of Africa developed very differently. It was isolated from most of the world. South of the Sahara, contacts between Africans and other continents were through distant and complicated trade routes. Therefore, those African cultures became very distinctive.

The contributions of early African cultures south of the Sahara were unique and important. It was in West Africa, the large bulge of Africa above the equator, that a number of the earliest and richest cultures arose.

Chapter

2 Great Empires in West Africa

Once the great desert began to form in the center of West Africa, many of the Saharan people moved south and lived either in the forests of the lower Niger River or in the grasslands of the upper Niger. Between 500 B.C. and A.D. 1500, powerful kingdoms developed in the two regions with well-developed governments, strong educational systems, religious customs, and organized cities. They were skillful in metalworking, trade, agriculture, and the arts.

The rich cultures that rose in West Africa built on each other, each one advancing the knowledge and skills developed by the previous one. They also learned new ideas through elaborate trading networks linking them with each other and with groups outside their region. Scientists believe that the earliest organized and skilled cultures to develop after the climate change in the Sahara were in the forests of Nigeria.

Although Nok craftsmen sculpted imaginative terra-cotta figures (pictured), their use of early forms of bronze and iron making marked the beginning of the age of metals in Africa.

The Metalworkers of Nigeria

In 1944 tin miners in what is known today as central Nigeria discovered thousands of clay fragments and some small sculptures in layers of the mine. Scientists who examined the discoveries named the early clay-working culture Nok, after a nearby mining village. Farmers and skilled craftsmen living between 1000 B.C. and A.D. 600, the Nok people existed at the same time as the ancient Greek civilization, with its highly developed architecture, literature, and government. Little is known about the Nok, but their imaginative terra-cotta, or clay, figures are evidence of a well-developed culture. Some were life-size and required great skill in firing to harden the clay figures. Early forms of bronze and iron making also developed among the Nok. These skills were a great advancement over those of the Stone Age Saharan people and marked the beginning of the age of metals in Africa.

The Ife and Benin Cultures

Many Yoruba-speaking groups lived in the lower Niger River area after the Nok culture, trading with one another. The most important Yoruba religious and cultural center was at Ife, ruled by a much-revered king. Building on the Nok culture in the A.D. 1200s, the Ife people introduced advanced metalwork such as bronze and brass casting.

It was the final Nigerian culture of Benin, however, that turned bronze casting into a high art form. A prosperous community near the Niger River delta on the Atlantic coast, ancient Benin flourished in the 1450s and produced many important products. Its ironwork, weapons, wood carvings, and many types of vegetables were desired in other parts of Africa. Benin's rulers were good businessmen and developed a form of currency to replace the barter, or exchange, system. Archaelogists know more about the Benin culture because they have found existing cast bronze sculptures and decorative wall pieces. These pieces, which once furnished the palace of the king of Benin, or *oba*, record the history, festivals, and religion of the people.

With so many saleable products, the Benin people were eager to expand their trade with other parts of Africa. It was not surprising, then, that Benin traders were shipping their goods north to the upper Niger region, where a series of great trading empires arose.

Other African cultures developed along the upper Niger and Senegal Rivers, which flowed through the Sahel, a region on the southern edge of the Sahara Desert. These cultures gained power and wealth because of their location at the center of the trade network of West Africa.

Agriculture was difficult in the Sahel region, so the people of the Sahel were dependent on trade. Fortunately, since gold was found in small deposits scattered throughout West Africa, they were able to

Following in the footsteps of the Nok and Ife cultures, the Benin people turned bronze casting into a high art form. This bronze plaque depicts three men holding small gourdlike rattles.

Benin City

After the decline of the kingdom of Benin, the ruins of Benin City were still impressive. Europeans who entered Benin City in the 1800s described what they saw, as recorded in Kingdoms of Africa *by Peter Garlake.*

"[There is] only a straggling collection of houses, built in clusters here and there, in little or no order. The number of ruins testified to the fact that it was once very much larger. [The palace was] entered through a doorway, the big door of which is lined with sheets of brass with stamped figures of men and leopards' heads. . . . On the other side of the compound . . . the wall is partly roofed in, and along this is a row of brass heads, and on top of every head is a long, heavy weather-worn, finely carved ivory tusk. Between the brass heads are brass castings of men on horseback, in armour of chain mail.

All the rafters are of wood carved with rough figures; some of the rafters have been covered with brass sheeting on which figures have been punched. The roof is supported by over 100 pillars of bronze sheets riveted together, giving a very good effect."

use it to trade for necessities. Archaeologists describe the way gold was mined at that time:

People were farmers and gained their living from their crops and lands. However, the soils of many goldfields were infertile, and their yields [harvests] were poor. Many months of the year were rainless. There was no work in the fields during those months. Farmers then turned to mining, gambling with the hope of a lucky strike. Single families or small temporary groups came together in a mining venture.

None of the fields was rich. [Gold] lay near the bottom of deep deposits of river sands and gravels. To get it, shafts up to 60 feet deep had to be sunk. Even with this effort, finding concentrations of the metal were extremely uncertain. Mining was difficult and dangerous work. Only the hope of a lucky strike made the effort worthwhile.[5]

The precious gold was used to trade for salt from Mediterranean coastal traders. Salt was prized as a treasure by the people of the Sahel, for it was needed in their diet. This mutually beneficial trade was accomplished by camel caravans, which made their way across the Sahara to the Sahel, bringing salt to trade for gold. Salt was mined under difficult conditions by small groups still living in the Sahara. A primary source of salt was in the central Sahara at Taghaza, an important stop on the caravan

Arab traders from eastern Africa and the Mediterranean coast were active in African trade routes and helped to expand the caravan network.

route. A Muslim traveler from Morocco named Ibn Battutah wrote a description of the salt city of Taghaza in the 1300s:

> [It is] an unattractive village, with the curious feature that its houses and mosques are built of blocks of salt, roofed with camel skins. There are no trees there, nothing but sand. In the sand is a salt mine. They dig for the salt and find it in thick slabs, lying one on top of the other, as though they had been tool-squared and laid under the surface of the earth.[6]

The gold and salt trade soon expanded to include other trade items as well, so that the people of the Sahel began to trade for fruits, ceramics, cloth, and tools with distant cultures in eastern Africa and the Mediterranean coast. Arab traders from these areas became active in the African trade routes, expanding the caravan network. The Arabs of the eastern Mediterranean countries governed all of North Africa and even Spain between A.D. 600 and 800. Adding the Saharan trade products to their businesses was very profitable.

One of the products the Arabs took with them wherever they went was their culture, its emphasis on education and the arts, and the religious beliefs of Islam. It was not long before Arab businessmen had moved into the African trade cities, and by A.D. 1000 Muslim culture and beliefs had been introduced into West Africa.

The distant but busy caravan trade helped the people of the Sahel prosper and develop large and powerful kingdoms called merchant empires. For hundreds of years each of these empires expanded and built on the one before it.

Ancient Ghana

Control of the caravan routes in West Africa was centered on a road system between the Muslim Arabs of North Africa, who brought salt, and the gold miners and traders of the Sahel. At this strategic hub of roads rose a powerful empire named Ghana. Ancient Ghana was located north of present-day Ghana, on a large wedge of land between the upper Niger and Senegal Rivers. It covered parts of today's Mali and Mauritania.

Abu Hamid al-Andalusi, an Arab traveler from Spain, visited Ghana and reported on the impressive trade of salt for gold that was making Ghana wealthy:

In the sands of that country is gold, treasure inexpressible. Merchants trade with salt for it, taking the salt on camels from the salt mines. They start from a town called Sijilmasa [ancient caravan oasis in today's Morocco] . . . and travel in the desert as it were upon the sea, having guides to pilot them by the stars or rocks. . . . They take provisions for six months, and when they reach Ghana, they weigh their salt and sell it against a certain unit of weight of gold . . . according to the market and the supply.[7]

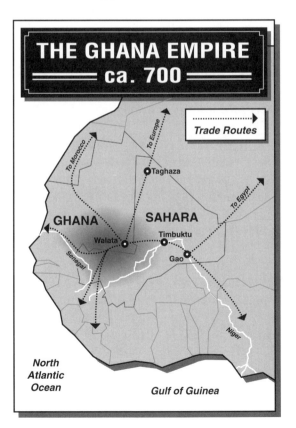

As the first great merchant empire, Ghana flourished between A.D. 700 and 1200, after the Nok culture and before the Benin culture. In their large cities built of stone, the people of Ghana were proud of their iron tools and weapons. Iron ore was widespread and easy to mine, and every village had its ironworkers. All trade was taxed, so the people of Ghana received copper, cloth, dried fruit, and other special goods as taxes from Arab traders. This made the markets of Ghana lavish with new products and interesting foods.

An early Arab explorer, Ibn Hawqal, wrote his *Book of Ways and Provinces* in the tenth century, which is excerpted in the *Horizon History of Africa.* In it he described the king of Ghana as "the wealthiest of all kings on the face of the earth on account of the riches he owns and the hoards of gold acquired by him and inherited from his predecessors since ancient times."[8]

Many merchants from the Middle East and North Africa moved to Ghana's cities and became an important influence. Some were Jewish, but most were Arab. The Muslim Arabs were forceful in their belief in Islam. However, the people of Ghana strongly resisted Muslim beliefs. They maintained their religious traditions that emphasized spirits in nature and reverence for ancestors.

The Rise of Mali

By A.D. 1200 Sundiata, a strong African military leader, and his large army had conquered Ghana and created the new kingdom of Mali. Sundiata's armies expanded Mali, and soon the empire stretched from the Atlantic coast across all the Senegal and upper Niger River basins. A trader described it as "Square in shape, being four months [of travel] in length and as much in breadth." As many as twelve thousand camels a year crossed just one of eight major Saharan trade routes, stopping at key oases for rest, water, and supplies. A trader wrote this letter to the merchant in Genoa, Italy, who had hired him:

After we had come from the sea . . . we journeyed on horseback, always southwards, for about twelve days. For seven days we encountered no dwelling—nothing but sandy plains; we proceeded as though at sea, guided by the sun during the day, at night by the stars. At the end of the seventh day, we arrived at a ksour [oasis] where dwelt very poor people who supported

Justice and Faithfulness in Mali

Ibn Battutah, a scholar and theologian from Tangier on the Mediterranean Sea, crossed the Sahara and spent about a year in the kingdom of Mali. Selections from his Travels in Asia and Africa: 1325–1354 *are included in* The African Past and the Coming of the European, *edited by Leon Clark. In* Travels, *Ibn Battutah recorded these observations about Mali.*

"Among the admirable qualities of these people, the following are to be noted:

1. The small number of acts of injustice that one finds there; for the Negroes are of all peoples those who most abhor injustice. The sultan [Muslim ruler] pardons no one who is guilty of it.

2. The complete and general safety one enjoys throughout the land. The traveler has no more reason than the man who stays at home to fear brigands [bandits], thieves, or ravishers.

3. The blacks do not confiscate the goods of white men (that is, of North Africans) who die in their country, not even when these consist of big treasures. They deposit them, on the contrary, with a man of confidence among the whites until those who have a right to the goods present themselves and take possession.

4. They make their [Muslim] prayers punctually; they assiduously [persistently] attend their meetings of the faithful, and punish their children if they should fail in this. On Fridays, anyone who is late at the mosque will find nowhere to pray, the crowd is so great. Their custom is to send their servants to the mosque to spread their prayer-mats in the due and proper place, and to remain there until they, the masters, should arrive."

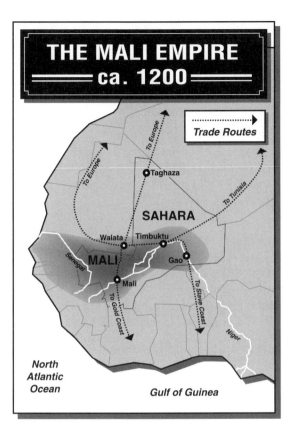

THE MALI EMPIRE
ca. 1200

Trade Routes

To Europe
To Europe
To Tunisia
Taghaza
SAHARA
Walata   Timbuktu
MALI   Gao
Senegal
Mali
To Gold Coast
To Slave Coast
Niger
North Atlantic Ocean
Gulf of Guinea

of Mali a new way of life based on the Koran, or Islamic holy book, with its own laws, system of taxation and justice, and commitment to scholarship and learning.

The Mali city of Timbuktu, in fact, became one of the most important educational centers. Located on the great northern bend of the Niger River, Timbuktu became a place of culture and learning. It was home to a Muslim university, many mosques and libraries, and handsome stone buildings. At the same time that Christian monks were copying manuscripts in stone monasteries in Europe, Muslim scholars from all over northern Africa traveled to Timbuktu to study. Its importance was known throughout western and northern Africa.

An early depiction of Timbuktu, an ancient Mali city. Timbuktu was renowned throughout western and northern Africa as a place of culture and learning.

themselves on water and a little sandy ground. . . .

This locality (oasis) is a mart [market] of the country of the Moors [Muslims], to which merchants come to sell their goods: gold is carried hither, and bought by those who come up from the coast . . . ; there are many rich men here. The generality, however, are very poor, for they do not sow, nor do they harvest anything, save the dates upon which they subsist.[9]

Mali controlled all trade between West Africa and Arab North Africa, but it was also important in other ways. The empire became known for its strong and just government and its rich culture based on Islamic ideas. Islam introduced to the people

Mali's fame spread to Europe when Sundiata's grandson, Mansa Musa, now emperor of Mali, made a pilgrimage to Mecca in Saudi Arabia in 1324. For a Muslim this was a very important journey to the most holy place in the Islamic world. Sixty thousand men, musicians, and columns of laden camels accompanied Mansa Musa on his pilgrimage. All across northern Africa the Mali ruler gave out gold to those he visited. Upon his arrival in Mecca, news of Mansa Musa's wealth and generosity had gone before him. Word of Mali's wealth spread throughout Europe. Mapmakers added the kingdom to their developing maps of Africa. In the 1300s Europe was emerging from the Middle Ages, a time of poverty, hardship, and little cultural development. Impressed by reports about Mali and its highly developed culture, European adventurers and scholars made plans to visit the exotic West African empire. When Mansa Musa died twenty-five years after his impressive pilgrimage, his great empire began to break apart, and other empires rose one at a time in its place.

Merchant Empires Spread

The empires that gained importance after Mali's influence declined attempted to increase their trade eastward. Wealthy trading cultures like the Songhay continued to impress foreign visitors. When Ibn Battutah visited Gao, capital of the Songhay empire, he declared, "[It] is one of the finest towns in the Negroland. It is also one of their biggest and best provisioned towns with rice in plenty, milk and fish."[10] The scholar named Leo Africanus also visited Gao and described it as a town full of "exceeding rich merchants; and hither continually resort great store of [to them come a great many] Negroes which buy cloth here brought out of Barbarie [North African coast] and Europe. . . . It is a wonder to see what plentie of Merchandize is dayly brought hither, and how costly and sumptuous all things be."[11]

Leo Africanus traveled on to Kanem-Bornu, a large empire near Lake Chad that was dependent on the profitable east-west caravan trade. Several groups were held together under the Kanuri kings, who maintained tight control of the region so that the empire could dominate the caravan trade. In his writings, Africanus described the king's disciplined followers:

> Horsemen he hath in a continuall readiness to the number of 3000 and an huge number of footmen; for all his subjects are so serviceable and obedient unto him [the king] that wherever he commandeth them, they will arme themselves and follow him whither he pleaseth to conduct them. They paye unto him none other tribute but the tithes [taxes] of all their corne; neither hath this king any revenues to maintaine his estate, but only such spoils as he getteth from his next enemies by often invasions and assaults."[12]

For eight hundred years the wealthy and powerful merchant empires ruled West Africa. In eastern Africa, however, cultures and empires rose that were very different from those in western Africa.

Chapter

3 The Glories of East Africa

In East Africa the rugged and difficult geography strongly influenced the development of its cultures, small and large. These cultures were also influenced by the nearness of the Egyptian Empire. The most important influence on East Africa, however, was the Arab Muslims. Once the Arabian empires sailed across the Red Sea, they had a lasting impact on East Africa. Because of these two nearby cultures, powerful and distinct societies arose in East Africa, and they were quite different from those in West Africa.

The Rise of Meroë

Those who sailed south from Egypt toward the upper Nile River had to overcome five great sets of rapids and falls, called cataracts. At the sixth cataract stood Meroë on a large island in the middle of the river. It was an elaborate city with monumental sculptures and small pyramid tombs, but it was not part of the Egyptian Empire. By 600 B.C., the same time period as the height of the ancient Nok in West Africa, Meroë was the capital of a rich, independent culture that adopted many Egyptian traditions. In fact, Meroë became so powerful that it briefly

ruled Egypt. Burials of Meroë's nobility included elaborate funeral offerings such as gold and alabaster items and human sacrifices. Seven queens were recorded on the monuments of Meroë. Powerful rulers,

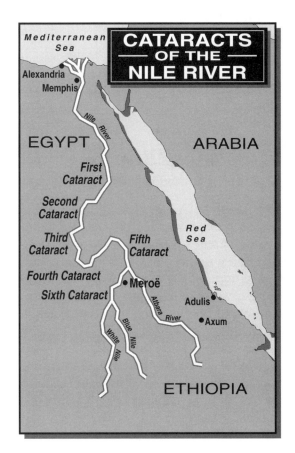

they were called *candace*, which means "queen" or "queen mother."

Meroë was best known as a center of ironmaking. Furnaces and remains from ironworking have been uncovered in the ruins of ancient Meroë. Archaeologists suspect that ironmaking skills spread from Meroë across the continent to the Nok people in Nigeria. The merchants of Meroë were also clever in developing their trade skills and adopted a form of hieroglyphic, or picture, writing for their records.

Meroë became the center of trade between the Mediterranean Sea and other parts of Africa. The city on the Nile may even have traded with countries as far away as China. Meroë traded ivory and skillful ceramics for gold with West Africa, over two thousand miles away.

Eventually Meroë declined because of the growing power of nearby Axum, which took over the rich trade routes that had bestowed such renown and riches on Meroë.

Ethiopian Axum

The people of Axum were different from the people of Meroë. Descended from Arab farmers who had sailed across the Red Sea long ago, they developed a culture completely separate from the influence of Egypt. Around A.D. 300 Axum conquered Meroë and took its place as the trade center of northeastern Africa. The trade was now split three ways: between West Africa, the Mediterranean cultures, and the countries around the Indian Ocean. The active seaport of Adulis on the Red Sea was Axum's chief trade city. Axum's official language was Greek, since Axum traded with regions conquered by Greece's Alexander the Great. Axum's coins and historic monuments were inscribed with the Greek language.

In the year A.D. 1 a Greek writer created a sailor's and businessman's travel guide to parts of western Asia. It described the busy port of Adulis and the riches traded with the Axumite kingdom:

> Adulis [is] a fair-sized village, from which there is a three days' journey to Coloe, an inland town and the first market for ivory. From that place to Axum, the city of the people called Axumites, there is a five days' journey more. To that place all the ivory is brought from the country beyond the Nile.

> There are imported into these places . . . cloth made in Egypt for the Berbers; double-fringed linen mantles [cloaks]; many articles of flint glass and others of murrhine [a colored stone]; and brass, which is used for ornament and cut pieces instead of coin; sheets of soft copper, used for cooking utensils and cut up for bracelets and anklets for the women; iron, which is made into spears used against the elephants and other wild beasts, and in their wars.[13]

Early Axumite leaders built impressive tall and slender stone monuments called stelae, many of which mark tomb sites. Inscriptions on the stelae tell of Axumite rulers and their history. The Arab people who built the Axumite Empire were not Muslim, and when they developed trade with the Greek world, they became interested in Christianity. The kingdom of Axum became officially Christian around

Strange Reports from Meroë

The Roman emperor Nero sent the first recorded expedition to discover the source of the Nile River. The expedition's eyewitness account, as well as distorted rumors, was included in Natural History *by Pliny the Elder, written in the first century* A.D. *This excerpt from* Natural History *is included in a large volume edited by Alvin M. Josephy Jr.,* The Horizon History of Africa.

"The grass in the vicinity of Meroë becomes of a greener and fresher color, and there is some slight appearance of forests, as also traces of the rhinoceros and elephant. They reported also that . . . the buildings in the city were but few in number, and they stated that a female, whose name was Candace, ruled over the district, that name having passed from queen to queen for many years. They were informed that in the days of the Aethiopian dominion, the island of Meroë enjoyed great renown. According to tradition, it was in the habit of maintaining two hundred thousand armed men and four thousand artisans.

The whole of this country has successively had the names of Aetheria, Atlantia, and last of all, Aethiopia, from Aethiops, the son of Vulcan [Roman god of the forge]. It is not at all surprising that towards the extremity of this region the men and animals assume a monstrous form. . . . It is reported that in the interior, on the eastern side, there is a people that have no noses, the whole face presenting a plane surface; that others again are destitute of [without] the upper lip, and others are without tongues."

A.D. 450. The Christian culture was strengthened by monks who encouraged education, literature, and art and created distinctive religious architecture.

Eventually intense competition for trade developed between Ethiopia, as the land of Axum was called, and nearby Muslim Arab states. When the critical seaport of Adulis was destroyed by the Muslim Arabs, Ethiopians retreated into the mountainous interior of the country. They were forced to abandon their coastal trade to the powerful Arab states.

As the Ethiopian culture became isolated from the rest of the world, it retained its trade with interior and western Africa. The Ethiopians prospered in their mountain strongholds, fought off invaders, and strengthened their Christian traditions. Elaborate and unique Christian churches were hewn out of solid rock. Some were created below ground level, invisible above ground. At the threat of Muslim invasion, the churches could be totally hidden with earth and protected from destruction. Eight of these churches were lo-

The church of St. George—one of the Christian churches located at Lalibela—was built below ground level so it could be hidden with earth during Muslim invasions.

cated at Lalibela. The city was named after the beloved Christian king who ordered their construction in the twelfth century. Thus, Africans were building elaborate churches around the same time period that Christians were building large stone cathedrals in Europe.

For over two thousand years the Ethiopian Christian culture was repeatedly threatened by Arab invasions. The Ethiopian *Royal Chronicles* describe the defense of the kingdom in the 1300s by Emperor Amda Tseyon, or 'Amda Seyon.

> Meanwhile the Arab armies were advancing, every man armed, and in number they were as the stars of heaven and the sand of the sea-shore, and the rain clouds of the sky. As they marched the earth shook. The wild beasts were so terrified that they ran before them and took refuge in the camp of 'Amda Seyon. And the queen sent to 'Amda Seyon a quantity of Jordan [River] water and some dust from Golgotha. The king called the priest Takla Seyon and told him to baptize him with the water, as he stood there in full armor; and as the water fell upon him his weakness departed and the strength of God came upon him. And the king himself sprinkled his horses and his men with the water.

> The enemy were men of huge stature and wore their hair hanging down to their waists like women, and though they tied themselves to each other by means of their clothes so that no man might flee, they were conquered by the king. 'Amda Seyon remounted his horse and set out with his soldiers to cut down those who were fleeing, and meanwhile the Abyssinian women came out and stripped the dead and carried their weapons back to their camp. The battle dragged on for six hours until sunset, by which time the Muslims were either scattered or slain. . . . When the battle was over 'Amda Seyon returned to his camp, and entering his chapel gave thanks to God for his victory He had given him.[14]

In spite of the efforts of East African people to resist domination by Arab trading countries, all of the narrow coastline of eastern Africa was eventually settled by these traders. By 700 Muslim Arab merchants had established a new culture on coastal Africa.

The Power of the Zanj

As the merchant empire of Ghana was growing in strength in West Africa, the

Zanj culture took hold in eastern Africa. This Arab culture was rooted in the Muslim faith and supported by naval trade with much of Asia. Sturdy Zanj ships crisscrossed the Indian Ocean and even ventured as far as the South China Sea.

The hot lowland coast of East Africa is a narrow strip of land from Ethiopia to the large island of Madagascar. There are few natural harbors on the coast itself, but several of the off-shore islands are suitable for naval trade. Most of the East African people lived inland, so it was not difficult for Arab traders to establish trade stations along the coast. A history of the Zanj people was written in the *Chronicle of the Kings of Kilwa*, which details the history of the seaport kingdom of Kilwa. Although the actual *Chronicle* was lost, a Portuguese historian was able to save information from the *Chronicle* and rewrite it in his own words. He copied the story of the beginnings of the Zanj culture:

> As the land of Arabia is very close to these lands, the first foreign people who came to settle in the land of Zanzibar were a tribe of Arabs, who had been banished after adopting a sect of Muhammad. . . . After their arrival, they worked their way like a slow plague along the coast, taking possession of fresh settlements, until there arrived three ships with a large num-

Merchants sell their goods at a busy fruit market on the island of Zanzibar, a Zanj city located off the coast of Tanzania.

ber of Arabs in the company of seven brothers.

The first settlement they made in this land of Ajan [Zanj] was the city of Mogadishu [in Somalia] . . . which even at the present time is governed by twelve chiefs in the manner of a republic, and they are descendents of the seven brothers. Mogadishu so excelled in power and statesmanship that it became overlord and capital of all the Moors [Negro Muslims] of this coast.[15]

The merchants at major trade centers like Kilwa became very wealthy by taxing the exchange of goods between East African Zanj traders and ships from countries all around the Indian Ocean. From Africa, goods such as gold, ivory, iron, and tortoiseshell were purchased by Arab traders. Slaves captured by Arab traders from inland Africa were also important exchange items. All African goods were traded for textiles and jewelry from India and silk and porcelain from China. The Zanj also valued foodstuffs such as wheat, rice, sesame oil, and honey.

Kilwa was on a tiny island off the coast of Tanzania. Its impressive living complexes were an indication of the luxurious life of wealthy Zanj citizens. Elegant three- and four-story houses were made from

Great Zimbabwe's Extensive Trade Network

In his book, The Kingdoms of Africa, *Peter Garlake reports on the archaeological evidence indicating that Great Zimbabwe's trade included goods from as far away as Syria, the Persian Empire, and China.*

"A unique hoard of the most diverse and bizarre goods was unearthed in 1902 in an enclosure just outside the largest ruin. . . . There was a great quantity of coiled wire of iron, copper, bronze and gold; sheets and beads of gold; ingots of copper; and copper jewelry. Three iron gongs . . . were found. These are characteristic musical instruments of West Africa.

With them was a small but extraordinary group of foreign bangles. Many of these are of types that have never been found anywhere else in the interior. There was an iron spoon, an iron lampstand, bits of coral, [European] bronze hawk bells, copper chains, cowrie shells, engraved and enameled Syrian glass, a Persian bowl bearing an Arabic inscription, Chinese vessels. There were also tens of thousands of glass trade beads. . . . Whatever it was, it is a striking illustration of Great Zimbabwe's preeminence as a center of trade, of tribute and of industry on the plateau."

stone and coral. Arab and African architects would first cut the soft sea coral into building blocks and then allow the blocks to harden in the sun. Coral refuse was then ground into powder for mortar to hold the blocks together and for plastering the walls. Archaeologists have confirmed the elegance of Kilwa's leaders by studying the palace remains of a Zanj Muslim sultan.

Husumi Kubwa, meaning "large fortified house," is a group of pavilions set around courtyards. There are both public and private rooms, store rooms, an octagonal bathing pool, and a small mosque separate from the rest but connected by a staircase. The buildings were beautifully decorated with elaborate stone carvings. There is an outer wall that seems to be part of a fortification [along the edge of the sea]. Sailboats brought visitors and traders to the palace.[16]

Kilwa was just one of a string of seaport cities the Zanj established along the East African coast. Many of the Zanj cities remain today and are familiar names: Malindi and the islands of Mombasa and Lamu of Kenya; Mogadishu, the capital of Somalia; Zanzibar, a large island off Tanzania; and Sofala, a seaport of Mozambique. A twelfth-century document reported on the gold trade of Sofala:

This settlement, which the Moors had made in this place called Sofala, was not made by force of arms, nor against the will of the natives of the land, but by their wish and that of the prince who ruled at the time; because by reason of this intercourse [exchange] they obtained benefits as well as cloth and other things which they had never

had before, and for which they gave gold and ivory, which was of no use to them, and which, until then, had never been exported from Sofala. And although this barbarous race never left the village in which they were born, and were not given to navigation, nor to travel by land in pursuit of commerce, gold nevertheless has this quality, namely, that wherever it is found on earth, the report of it spreads from one person to another so that they go to find its place of origin.[17]

Great Zimbabwe

The gold trade funneled through Sofala and into the Zanj ships from Great Zimbabwe, a wealthy inland trading center. Located on a strategic plateau between the large Zambezi and Limpopo Rivers, the Zimbabwe highlands were rich with minerals. The city had fertile land and was near both forests and savannas, or grasslands. The people of Zimbabwe were good farmers, herders, craftspeople, and metalworkers. After the harvest whole families panned for gold during the dry season, but they also mined iron and copper, which they made into pots and household and luxury items. Archaeologists have found much evidence of Great Zimbabwe's productive population:

Gold, copper and iron were worked. Crucibles [melting pots] and the tools used in drawing metal into the thin wire needed for bangles and bracelets have been found in deposits in the [ruins]. Gold beads, gold wire and thin sheets of gold, used to cover

The ruins of Great Zimbabwe, a wealthy trading center. At the height of its civilization, over two hundred stone compounds covered the Zimbabwe highlands.

wooden carvings, were found in abundance. Nodules [small lumps] of iron ore were found on the floor of a cave. There were the remains of smelting furnaces nearby. Soapstone was carved to make flat, wide dishes. Their sides were decorated with carved cable patterns or long-horned cattle, zebras or baboons. . . . Cotton was spun and presumably woven, to judge by the many spindle whorls [spinning tool]. . . . It is unlikely that cotton was grown locally. It may have come from as far afield as the Zambezi River valley.[18]

The construction of Great Zimbabwe was very impressive. *Zimbabwe* means "royal court" in the Shona language, and *great zimbabwe* can also be interpreted as "great stone house." Huge, carefully laid stone walls, some thirty feet high and eight hundred feet in circumference, cir-

cled the living compounds. All the compounds were called *zimbabwes*, but one especially large one featured an intricately constructed conical stone tower that rose high above its walls. Another series of *zimbabwes* had large carved stone birds, The Bird of God, placed on tops of columns.

Over two hundred stone compounds covered the highland center of Great Zimbabwe, and an elaborate drainage system was built into the site. It is estimated that around ten thousand people lived in Great Zimbabwe in traditional thatch houses. Some lived within the stone compounds, but most people lived outside of them.

As in West Africa, prosperity and cultural development in East Africa were clearly linked to trade routes and trading partners. This pattern of growth and development did not occur for the large forest kingdoms that developed in the huge interior of Africa.

Chapter

4 Tradition in Central and Southern Africa

The ancient people of central and southern Africa were either small village dwellers or nomads. Nomads built temporary villages as they followed their herds to good grazing land. The huge mass of Africa below the western bulge of the continent was their home, a territory twice the size of the United States. It was a diverse land isolated by its geography and climate. Contact with cultures outside the continent was prevented for centuries. No Arab ships ventured past the dangerous Cape of Good Hope at the southernmost tip of the continent to the west coast of Africa. No trading empire to the north sought its markets. Overland contact among peoples in other parts of the continent was minimal. For centuries the villagers and nomads of central and southern Africa developed uniquely African societies and traditions untouched by European or Middle Eastern influence.

The Congo River Basin

Located in the very heart of Africa, the Congo River basin was home to a huge population of fishermen and farmers. The basin is so enormous that it is equal to about one-half the size of the United

States; six African countries today share land in this area. Its dense tropical forest sits astride the equator. A widespread complex of rivers drains into the two thousand-mile-long Congo River before it empties into the Atlantic Ocean. The plentiful rainfall, network of rivers, and abundant wildlife are able to support many people.

While the benefits of the Congo River basin nurtured countless villages, its obstacles prevented trade with societies outside the basin. Then, as now, the tropical forest was so dense and thick that overland travel was difficult. Transporting trade goods was a great challenge. The rivers of the basin were little help, for they were narrow rushing rivers forced through gorges and over countless waterfalls. Fishermen sailed small boats on short stretches of the rivers, but transporting people or produce over long distances was an overwhelming task. When outsiders entered the tropical forest in the late 1400s, they learned how this world isolated its inhabitants:

Uregga, it appears, occupies a broad belt of country lying north-east and south-west. Its people know nothing of the immediate settlements contiguous [next] to them, and though within twenty miles of the Luabal [River],

Without the influence of European and Middle Eastern cultures, people living in the Congo River basin developed societies and traditions that were uniquely African.

many adult males had never seen it. They have been imprisoned now for some five or six generations within their almost impenetrable forest fastnesses [remote places], and the difficulty of traveling, and the danger that would be incurred unless they united in strong bands, are the causes of their knowing nothing of the world outside, and the outside world knowing nothing of them.[19]

Traditional Village Life

While there were differences among them, the Congo basin villages shared many traditions. In order to survive, village cultures were carefully organized societies. Loyalties to family and religious beliefs were most important. Village religious centers were not buildings, but rather certain natural sites revered as sacred. The village preserved the important religious stories about these holy places. They were often unique land formations like caves, springs, or unusual mountains. This reverence for special sites was similar to the beliefs of the ancient Greeks and Romans living during the same time period. The Greeks honored the gods living on Mount Olympus and treasured numerous sacred springs as holy sites.

In most village cultures the gods were spirits that dwelled in all living things.

Trees, rivers, mountains, and animals all had spirits. There was usually one high god, or supreme spirit, often viewed as the creator of the world. Spirits were worshipped in special ceremonies developed through the centuries. Often, costumed figures in masks representing the spirits had special roles during the ceremonies. Offerings such as fruits, vegetables, or animals were dedicated to the spirits. Sometimes the food was cooked like a meal, and sometimes the animal was sacrificed as an offering. The ancient Greeks and Romans also worshipped their gods in much the same way.

Africans believed that the spirits of the dead continued to remain in the village, especially spirits of those who had recently died. It was important to ensure the happiness of all spirits, especially those of the dead. Offerings were carefully made, and family and village cooperation was enforced. If people harmed the village or family through selfishness or meanness, the spirits would be angered. Illness and bad luck would inflict village members. Therefore, cooperation and obedience were highly valued within the village.

Religious leaders were usually elders or members of a certain family designated

In traditional African villages, certain natural sites were revered as holy places. In the Congo basin, villagers held numerous ceremonies at these religious centers.

to be priests, the guardians of sacred traditions. When a group of villages gathered together under the leadership of a single ruler or king, that ruler frequently became the high priest or was even regarded as a god himself. This was a position of both privilege and great responsibility. The destiny and prosperity of the society rested on the shoulders of the rulers and religious leaders. Everyone's well-being depended on the leaders' wisdom.

Music, Dance, and the Arts

Village ceremonies always included traditional singing, dancing, and drumming. Used also as a form of communication, drumming was an effective way of sending messages across difficult terrain. Many other kinds of musical instruments were also used, made of metals, forest and ocean products, and animal parts. Gongs, rattles, bells, and xylophones were made from iron, gourds, pottery, shells, wood, bones, and skins. Trumpetlike instruments were created from animal tusks and horns, while whistles and flutes came from clay, bamboo, wood, and horn. Stringed instruments could be plucked or played with a bow, with a gourd or wooden box as a sound chamber.

Traditional arts and architecture reflected the environment in which the people lived and the materials available to them. Thatched or woven grasses, reeds, or other plant fibers provided conical

How Accurate Is Oral History?

A Hungarian researcher discovered the accuracy of the oral tradition in the early 1900s when he recorded this account at a village hundreds of miles up the Congo River. It is included in The African Past and the Coming of the European, *edited by Leon Clark.*

"As the elders were talking of the great events of various reigns and we came to the 98th chief, Bo Kama Bomanchala, they said that nothing remarkable had happened during his reign except that one day at noon the sun went out, and there was absolute darkness for a short time.

When I heard this I lost all self-control. I jumped up and wanted to do something desperate. The elders thought that I had been stung by a scorpion.

It was only months later that the date of the eclipse became known to me . . . the 30th of March, 1680, when there was a total eclipse of the sun, passing exactly over Bushongo . . . ; there was no possibility of confusion with another eclipse, because this was the only one visible in the region during the 17th and 18th centuries."

Villagers cover their traditional dome-shaped homes using mats of woven grasses. These huts were easily repaired and stayed cool and dry in the hot, rainy climate.

roofs and rounded house walls. Some groups used clay for walls and skins for roofing. All of these houses were cool and dry and easily repaired or replaced, perfect for a hot, rainy climate. The houses were not large, for most daily activity like cooking and craft work occurred outdoors, in family courtyards, or village work areas.

While West Africans and East Africans created their arts from brass, bronze, stone, and ceramics, the inland villages developed arts primarily of wood. Wood was abundant and easy to fashion. Carved, scraped, decorated, and sculpted wooden arts filled the villages. Iron axes made it easier to shape ceremonial stools, elaborate headdresses, and spirit images. Honored in their community, wood-carving families carefully trained each generation of carvers.

A kneeling woman supports the seat of this ornately carved stool from the Luba culture. In many inland villages of Africa, wood carving was a revered art form.

Luba and Lunda Kingdoms

Since village leaders carried so much responsibility, they were viewed as special beings. As some leaders became stronger, they exerted influence over groups of villages, becoming kings. By the 1300s powerful rulers began to dominate larger and larger groups of villages, creating kingdoms. In the region of Katanga, the very center of the African continent, a collection of villages was formed into the Luba kingdom. Village chiefs served under a single king who had godlike stature. The king inherited his position from a designated sacred family. A second large kingdom was formed, the Lunda, and

eventually the two were joined into one great empire that covered most of what we know today as Zaire.

Elaborate wood carvings and woven palm cloth were special products of the Lunda. From this empire also came literary masterpieces like the Mwindo epic, a long adventure story about the Lunda hero, Mwindo. It was passed on through the carefully memorized oral tradition so that each generation could hear the precise version. In 1956 an American who lived and taught in the former Belgian Congo recorded this important epic:

> By that time he had become well acquainted with Nyanga people and their culture, and had learned that they had a special type of adventure story, known generically as "karisis," or epic text, which he had previously heard only in confused or fragmentary form.
>
> In the Kisimba region he visited the village of Bese in a dense rain forest known as Ibimbi. At Bese he met "she-karisi," [maker of an epic text] who agreed to recite the Mwindo epic for him. For twelve consecutive days the bard [singer-poet] narrated, sang and enacted the many episodes of the tale while Professor Bichwyck and his aides wrote it down verbatim.[20]

Living in the Great Rift Valley

To the east of the Congo River basin was the Great Rift Valley, with its many lakes and fertile valleys to attract fishermen and farmers. The high mountain ranges between the Rift Valley and the Congo River basin were a formidable barrier to migration and ongoing contact, so the people of the Rift Valley were also isolated from outside contacts.

The Great Rift Valley was formed by a ripping motion when large land masses pulled apart. Around 40 million years B.C. the eastern coast of Africa experienced violent change and pulled away from the rest of the continent. It left behind a very long, steep-sided valley filled with volcanos. The valley filled with a huge inland sea which drained and refilled several times over thousands of years.

Stretching from the Red Sea coast of Ethiopia through the mountains of Uganda, Kenya, and Tanzania, the Great Rift Valley finally ends in southeast Africa in Mozambique. It is named the Great Rift because it is the longest rift valley in the world.

During the same year that the Sahara was drying up, the waters of the Rift Valley also shrank into remnant lakes. The land

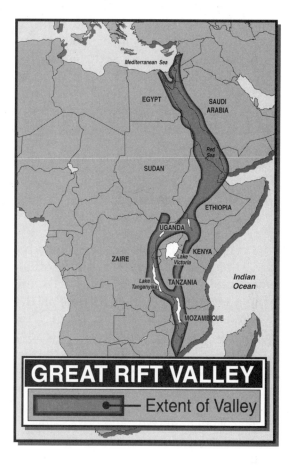

GREAT RIFT VALLEY

Extent of Valley

Extending from northern Ethiopia to southern Mozambique, the Great Rift Valley is abundant with lakes, lush valleys, and high mountain ranges.

around Lake Victoria, one of the largest lakes in the world, was heavily populated with traditional fishing settlements for thousands of years. Farmers like the Kikuyu preferred the fertile highlands with their predictable rainfall and rich volcanic soil, like the highlands of Uganda, Kenya, and Tanzania.

Nomadic Life

The rugged terrain of the valley floor became home to independent groups of nomadic cattle herders. The nomads like the Maasai created temporary villages on the savanna and moved with their herds. Nomadic life was highly structured in order to maintain group stability. Hundreds of years of traditions are evident in modern Maasai nomadic life. This personal account from Tanzania describes the traditional role of a nine-year-old boy:

> When Naikosai was sick, I started herding the flock of sheep and goats by myself. It was difficult and lonely, but I learned about animals by observing their behavior in unusual situations. One time when I was herding the flock in a dry riverbed, clouds started forming far and near. I imagined the thunder and lightning, which so often splits trees. As soon as it began to rain, the women of the kraal [village] would usually rush out to stop leaks in the houses by plastering them with cow dung. That done, they would then make sure the fire was burning so that when the wet shepherds returned from grazing their herds they could warm themselves and get dry.

The rain seemed endless. My limbs were shaking so that I started to feel tired and wanted to sit, but could not. My father had also warned me against that, because flock thieves are usually very active when it rained. So I walked around the herd and kept a watchful eye, occasionally shouting to make my presence known and to keep predators away, as my father had instructed me.

I prayed for the rain to stop and for the sun to set so I could drive the flock home. I cursed the rain but soon asked God to forgive my outburst, which was unbefitting a Maasai, for rain irrigates the dry land and the plain turns green for our cattle.

After herding on a rainy day, one is always anxious to return home. I thought of a warm, dry house, for darkness was approaching. I had often been fascinated to hear the elders counting days in relation to the color and appearance of the moon. For instance, the Maasai attack their enemies when the moon appears red and not green; they neither move camp nor perform any ceremonies when the moon is dead. During moonlit nights Maasai children play among the sleeping herd. On the night [of the rainy day], the moon was not visible and I and my age mates gathered around the fire to listen to stories of legendary heroes of Maasailand.[21]

Most groups living in the Great Rift Valley lived in small traditional clusters. The only structured kingdoms that emerged in the area were in the Ugandan highlands. A large state called Kitara de-

Traditional Maasai Wisdom

In his autobiography, The Worlds of a Maasai Warrior, *Tepilit Ole Saitoti recalls one of many stories told to the children to teach them to respect their parents and obey them without question.*

"Once upon a time a certain old man felt he was about to die, so he called all his sons to divide all his wealth among them. He distributed all his property to his sons, forgetting to give anything to one son who was very quiet by nature. This son then said, 'What about me, Father?' The old man answered, 'Son, there is nothing left except this cooking pot, and I will bless and give it to you.'

The son accepted the pot without complaining. Whenever warriors went to a slaughtering camp, they would borrow the cooking pot from the boy, and the agreement was that the boy would always accompany whoever borrowed the pot. At the camp feasts the boy ate well and grew faster and healthier than his brothers.

One day after a slaughter a warrior accidently damaged the pot with a spear. The boy cried loudly with grief, saying, 'You pierced my belly!' The warrior gave the boy a two-year-old calf, which was equivalent to the price of the pot.

It wasn't long before something happened to the boy's calf. A war was going on, and warriors heading to battle had gathered a large herd of calves for their food along the way. By chance the boy's calf wandered among the warriors' herd and was slaughtered. When the war was over, every Maasai warrior who took part in the war was required to give the boy a calf as payment for his loss, and the boy became richer than any of his brothers. This happened because he had accepted the cooking pot as the only inheritance from his father, without resentment."

veloped, which eventually was divided into two smaller kingdoms. One kingdom, Buganda, numbered about one million people, who raised bananas and cattle. The second kingdom was a fishing community established near Lake Victoria. In each kingdom the kings served as high priests and were considered sacred heroes, with all religious traditions centered on them. From these two kingdoms came the modern central African nations of Uganda, Rwanda, and Burundi.

The pattern of traditional villages and nomadic groups, loosely associated into family groups, included southern Africa. Just as in central Africa, difficult geography and climate were obstacles to trade or communication beyond southern Africa.

Southern Africa

South of the Congo River basin, the land rises steeply into dry highlands. The rain-bearing winds come from the east and drop their moisture along the eastern lands. Only the eastern third and extreme southern tip of Africa have fertile soil and climates suitable for agriculture. In the western half of southern Africa, there are forbidding deserts: the Namib, in today's Namibia, and the Kalahari, in today's Botswana. Flowing east to the Pacific Ocean are two great rivers, the Zambezi and Limpopo. The Zambezi was difficult to navigate, full of rapid currents and waterfalls. In the mid-1500s, a Portuguese Roman Catholic priest was the first European to report extensively on the Zambezi River:

The River Cuama is by them called Zambeze. The head whereof is so farre within Land that none of them know it. By tradition . . . it comes from a Lake in the midst of the Continent, which yields also other great Rivers. . . . It hath a strong current, and is in divers [various] places more than a league broad [seventy-two feet].

Mankala: A Game of Peace

Mankala *has been popular for so long in Africa that there are legends about various famous* mankala *players. The game is even important in the history of Zaire as a peaceful solution discovered by the Congolese king Shamba Bolongongo. This story appears in* African Crafts *by Jane Kerina.*

"Shamba Bolongongo was the 93rd Bushongo king who ruled at the height of the Bushongo Empire over 300 years ago. He was a philosopher, a moralist and a man of peace. In his day, he was known as a great inventor. King Shamba traveled widely around the continent seeking new ideas and creating new inventions for his people. He introduced the oil palm—which is named after him—to the Bushongo. He also brought his people the cassava and tobacco plants. He taught them new crafts such as raffia weaving.

It is said that when King Shamba came to power, his people had become a nation of gamblers, and there was much strife and bickering among them. It was important for the young ruler to restore harmony. He abolished gambling, and taught the people to play Mankala instead. Mankala has been a popular game ever since."

In order to survive in southern Africa, many traditional people became nomadic herders. These nomads were organized into family-related clusters that remained together while migrating to new pasture grounds.

They saile up this River West North-west above two hundred leagues, to the Kingdome of Sacumbe. [There] it makes a great Fall from Rockes, beyond which they goe up the River twentie leagues to the Kingdome of Chicova, in which are Mines of Silver, which cannot be sailed by reason of the strong current. From Chicova upwards it is Navigable, but how farre they know not.[22]

Some of the traditional people in southern Africa, like the San, or bushmen, adapted to the harsh desert conditions. Others like the Khoikhoi, or Hottentots, became nomadic herders, while the Kaffir, or Zulu, settled in the fertile eastern area.

Like the people of the Congo basin and the Great Rift Valley, the groups in southern Africa were isolated from outside contact for thousands of years. No complex kingdoms developed in the area, and the different groups maintained small, family-related clusters.

The isolation of thousands of years was not broken until the fifteenth century. When Europeans in search of exotic products and profit sailed down the full length of the African coast, they were willing to risk uncharted waters leading to unknown destinations. The appearance of Europeans on the shores of the African continent altered forever its stability, development, and prosperity.

Chapter
5 Sailing for Riches

In the 1400s, dramatic changes began to occur in the world that altered African life even up to this day. The Arab countries of the Middle East were at the heart of a very rich trade network, which Europeans were determined to claim as their own. At the same time, many African cultures in this network were at their pinnacle when their very existence was threatened by newcomers to their shores.

Seafarers Sent for Profits

For many years Europeans had sent traders overland to India and China to obtain prized spices, porcelain, and other treasures. This pattern changed when Arab countries in the Middle East took control of the overland trade routes, interfering with European trade profits. In response, seafaring countries like Spain and Portugal sent out explorers to find new ocean routes to the Indies as India, China, and the Asian islands were called. Spanish ships under Columbus went west hoping to reach the Indies, unaware that unknown continents blocked their path. The Portuguese, on the other hand, sent ships to sail around Africa to the desired markets of the Indies in hopes of finding an ocean route and bypassing the Arab trade network entirely.

Christopher Columbus's fleet plots a course for the Indies. Once Arab countries began to dominate overland trade routes, European countries were determined to find new ocean courses.

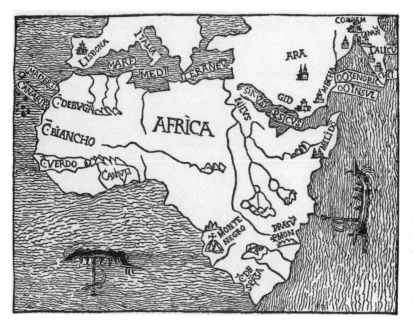

Portuguese ships routinely sailed around the hump of Africa to obtain treasures from the Indies. This woodcut from 1508 maps the journey around Africa's eastern and western coasts.

For centuries Arab traders had sailed and mapped the eastern coast of Africa, but no one had ever sailed down the western coast. In fact, European sailors looked at the uncharted Atlantic Ocean with fear, imagining all sorts of sea monsters and dreaded dangers. All of Africa south of the Sahara was a mystery, and only the caravan trade gave clues about African products and cultures.

With the new drive for profits, European navigators inched their ships little by little out of the Mediterranean Sea. When they made it around the hump of Africa, as the western bulge became known, they quickly learned that no new ocean horrors awaited them. In fact, they could obtain African gold, ivory, and other wonders more quickly by anchoring off the coast than by waiting for the slow camel caravans. By 1500 European trade ships were sailing regularly along the West African coast. It was closer for Africans to transport their trade goods to the coast, so

the long Saharan camel trade routes were no longer needed. The strategic location of the inland empires became meaningless, and the long West Africa coastline took on new importance.

Trade all along West Africa to the Congo River increased rapidly. Each year maps and sea charts became more and more accurate. Europeans then began to set up forts and trade stations at intervals along the coast.

First Contacts Peaceful

The first coastal contacts between Europeans and Africans were actually peaceful and conducted with mutual respect. They dealt with one another as equals, establishing trade contacts benefiting all. Neither group spoke the language of the other, so they communicated through gifts and ges-

Early English Trade with Africa

"The early trade of the English to the coast of Africa was very largely in exchange for products which could be sold in England. Among these may be mentioned elephants' teeth [tusks], wax, malaguetta and gold. . . . The hope of discovering gold mines was the principal cause of the first expedition sent to Africa by the Royal Adventurers in December, 1660. When this scheme to mine gold was abandoned, the company's agents traded for gold which was brought down from the interior or washed out by the slow and laborious toil of the natives. The other African products, especially elephants' teeth, were brought to London where they sold quite readily for very good prices."

In some areas trade was conducted without language for fifty years. Europeans were surprised by some of the sophisticated cultures of the West African coastline such as that of Benin. Samuel Blomert of Holland kept careful notes of his visit to Benin in 1720. Clearly Blomert considered the Benin culture to be on equal footing with his own, each having goods valued by the other:

> The King's palace occupies as much space as the [Dutch] town of Haarlem and is enclosed within walls. There are numerous apartments for the Prince's ministers, and fine galleries most of which are as big as those on the Exchange of Amsterdam. They are supported by wooden pillars encased with bronze, where their victories are depicted, and which are carefully kept very clean. . . .
>
> These Negroes are much more civilized than others on this coast. They are people who have good laws and a well-organized police; who live on good terms with the Dutch and other foreigners who come to trade among them, and to whom they show a thousand marks of friendship.
>
> [Agents of the king] visit the port magnificently dressed, wearing necklaces of jasper or fine coral. [They] offer greetings on behalf of their king, ask for news of Europe and of Holland, and distribute various fruits which the king sends with them.
>
> [They all] bargain as hard as they can, sometimes for whole months. [The Dutch buy] striped cotton garments which are retailed on the Gold Coast, and blue cloths which are sold on the rivers of Gabon and Angola, jasper

stones, leopard skins, pepper, and a few female slaves, for they refuse to sell men. [Those of Benin] buy cloth of red and silver, drinking vessels, all kinds of fine cottons, linen, red velvet, embroidered silk, coarse flannel; candied oranges, lemons and other green fruit; bracelets of brass, gilded mirrors, iron bars; and Indian cowries [shells] which serve as currency there.[23]

In fact, many African empires, including the Songhay people and the Kanem-Bornu people of the Sahel, were at their height. Europeans were not encountering uncivilized people, but rather highly cultured people. Muslim men were often scholars, more learned than most European sailors.

The Profitable Coast

Once Europeans traveled around Africa, parts of the West African coast were named for certain specialty products, such as the Pepper, or Grain, Coast; the Ivory Coast; the Gold Coast; and the Slave Coast. They were side by side on the lower coast of the West African hump, from today's Liberia to Nigeria and Cameroon.

The Portuguese were the first to round the hump and take advantage of the lucrative trade. Gold was their primary goal in the early 1500s. Rivals to the Portuguese, Dutch traders concentrated on the near west coast, around Senegal and Gambia. While Dutch ships also were busy sailing to the New World, Dutch traders seized Portuguese trade stations along the West African coast. By the mid-1600s competition was heating up, as Sweden, Denmark, England, France, and some of the German states sent ships to set up trade stations in the area. All were jostling for advantage in the lucrative trade. Strange and often distorted reports began to appear from visitors to this previously unknown Africa. From Englishman John Lok comes this account of his voyage in 1554 to an area known as Mina, a section of the coast of West Africa. Although hardly accurate, such accounts were popular in England. Lok also brought home an elephant's head, gold, and pepper.

It is to understand, that the people which now inhabit the regions of the

Foreigners vied for positions on Africa's profitable Grain, Ivory, Gold, and Slave coasts. This Danish fort was settled on the Gold Coast during the late 1600s.

coast of Guinea and the middle parts of Africa. As Lybia the inner and Nubia, with divers other great and large regions about the same, were in old time called Ethipes and Nigrite, which we now call Moors, Moorens, or Negroes. A people of beastly living, without a God, law, religion, or commonwealth, and so scorched and vexed with the heat of the sun that in many places they curse it when it riseth.[24]

As early as 1482 the first Portuguese explorers dropped anchor at the mouth of the Congo River. There they found a large and thriving kingdom called Kongo, or Congo, with a capital city, a royal court, and an efficient government. In 1491 the king was baptized a Christian, after which he exchanged ambassadors with the pope and the king of Portugal. King Nzinga Mbemba was described by a European visitor:

> The King of Congo, when hee goeth to the Campe to see his Armie, rideth upon an Elephant in great pompe and majestie, on either side of the Elephant he hath six slaves two of them were Kings, that he himselfe had taken in the field. . . . Then there followeth a More [Negro] which doth nothing but talke aloud in praise of the King, telling what a great Warriour he hath beene, and praising his wisdome for all things that hee hath accomplished.[25]

Once trade was established with the kingdom of Congo, ships ignored the West African coast past the Congo River. No rivers emptied into the ocean, and the barren coast and desert land visible from shore displayed none of the promise of the thriving Gold Coast area. Besides, the ultimate goal of the European sea captains was to sail completely around Africa to the treasures of the Indies. Learning to navigate the treacherous coastline and dangerous weather of the tip of Africa was quite a task.

First Bartholomew Dias in 1488 and then Vasco da Gama in 1497 threaded their way around the Cape of Good Hope for the glory of Portugal. Da Gama was astonished to discover the flourishing Zanj Empire on the eastern coast of Africa. Nothing like it existed on the other coastline. The Zanj were as powerful as the Portuguese, and they controlled the gold trade of the east coast, with Kilwa as their greatest trade center. From the *Chronicle of the Kings of Kilwa* comes this report of the coastal gold trade:

In 1497, the Portuguese explorer Vasco da Gama sailed around the treacherous Cape of Good Hope on the southern tip of Africa.

In 1602 Amsterdam businessmen could buy Description of Guinea, *a book that included the accounts of many travelers to West Africa. This selection describing Benin is included in Basil Davidson's* African Kingdoms.

"The city is very great when you go into it [for] you enter a great broad street, not paved, which seems to be seven or eight times broader than the Warmoes street in Amsterdam. It goes straight in and never bends. [Other great streets] open off the main street and you cannot see to the end of them because of their great length.

The houses stand in good order, one close and even beside the other as the houses in Holland stand. Those belonging to men of quality and others have two or three steps to go up, and along the front of them there is a kind of gallery [covered porch] where you may sit in the dry.

The king's court is very big, having within it many wide squares [courtyards] with galleries round them where watch is always kept. I went so far within these buildings that I passed through four such squares, and wherever I looked I still saw gate after gate which opened into other places."

The first people on this coast who came to the land of Sofala [in Mozambique] in search of gold were inhabitants of the city of Mogadishu [in Somalia]. In the course of time by means of the trade which the Moors [Muslims] had . . . , the kings of Kilwa became absolute masters of the gold trade. [King] Daut reigned at Kilwa for forty years and was succeeded by his son . . . who conquered the greater part of the coast. With his father's support, he became master of the trade of Sofala . . . and a large part of the mainland coast. Besides being a conqueror, he beautified the city of Kilwa, erecting there a fortress of stone and lime, with walls, towers and other houses, whereas up till that time nearly the whole of the dwellings in the city had been made of wood.[26]

Once the eastern coast was opened to Europeans, a stream of Portuguese ships rounded the southern tip of Africa to face the power of the Zanj.

East Coast Rivalry

Beautiful architecture and overflowing markets in the Zanj cities and trading ports impressed the Portuguese. Portuguese sailors marveled at Kilwa's fine, large houses "like those of Spain. In this land there are rich merchants and there is much gold and silver and amber and musk [perfume] and pearls. Those of the land wear clothes of fine cotton and of silk and many fine things, and they are black men."[27]

In fact, they were shocked that no one was interested in Portuguese trade goods like cotton, iron, copper, beads, and bells. The Zanj market goods already exceeded the Portuguese in quality. As reports of Zanj wealth filtered back to Portugal, the merchants backing the expensive trade ships making their way around Africa decided that it was essential to seize control of the Zanj trade. A few peaceful trade arrangments were made, but most were violent. Portuguese ships came heavily armed with guns and cannon. They proceeded to bombard coastal towns into submission. While some cities were forced only to pay taxes to the Portuguese, others were attacked, burned, and looted.

Control of the eastern African coastline was much prized, so power struggles continued for centuries. The Portuguese needed control so that they could set up supply stations for their trade ships on their way to the Indies. By 1510 the Portuguese had devastated the Zanj, but before long the Turks challenged their position. About seventy years later, Africans of the Zimba tribal group swept up the coast from the Zambezi River to Malindi in Kenya, killing everyone in their path. The Portuguese regained their power in the area for a while, building a major fort at Mombasa, Kenya. A Muslim revolt against the Portuguese at Mombasa brought quick support from Arab states to the north. The Portuguese were forced to withdraw from their strongholds, and Arab control returned to much of eastern coastal Africa by 1670.

When the Portuguese first sailed around southern Africa, they made no attempt to establish a supply station on the

The Dutch were the first to install supply stations on the Cape of Good Hope in southern Africa. These installations allowed voyagers to bypass the Portuguese-controlled East African coast.

Dutch pioneers were the first Europeans to colonize South Africa, establishing a supply station and farming settlement (pictured) near Cape Town.

stormy and forbidding coast. Instead, they used Zanj seaports of the East African coast for supplies. The importance of the East African coast dwindled after Dutch voyagers planted permanent supply stations on the tip of southern Africa. By relying on these stations, British and French ships found they could sail directly to India, avoiding the Portuguese-controlled East African coast.

Dutch Pioneers in South Africa

The first Europeans to permanently settle in Africa south of the Sahara were Dutch. By the mid-1600s a Dutch supply station near today's Cape Town, South Africa, be-

came a permanent settlement of Dutch farmers known as Boers. The settlement grew, and the native people of the area found themselves either pushed into the desert region or enslaved. African people in southern Africa resisted toiling for the Europeans. Therefore, the Boers imported slaves from Asia and India, called coloreds, to work their land.

The Dutch use of slaves foretold the transformation of the European and African trade. The one crucial product that soon took priority in African trade was slaves. Both coasts of Africa had a busy and successful trade in gold, ivory, and other luxury products. However, it was the mushrooming, immensely profitable slave trade that changed all trade relations between Europe and Africa and destroyed African cultures.

6 The Impact of the Slave Trade

The very first contacts between European voyagers and African people included slave trading. The roots of the gigantic European slave trade of the 1700s and 1800s began with the first explorers. By 1500 slaves were Africa's most valued commodity. An ancient slave trade had existed for centuries within Africa. However, that slave trade was significantly different from that of the Europeans. It took several centuries to untangle the complex web that made slavery so popular and profitable for so many people.

African and Arab Slave Trade

African cultures had captured and exchanged slaves among themselves for centuries, but they had different standards for

Although an ancient slave trade existed in Africa for hundreds of years, Europeans radically changed the trade and deprived slaves of freedoms they would have had in Africa.

Arab dealers gather as African slaves are paraded through a busy marketplace in Zanzibar. For centuries, a booming Arab slave trade existed on the east coast of Africa.

slaveholding from the Europeans. In Africa slaves were servants, but even the lowest slave might lead a caravan or own a slave. Among the Ashanti of the Gold Coast, slaves could marry, own property, and even inherit some of their master's property. An excellent example of the treatment of slaves among Africans comes from the autobiography of Olaudah Equiano. He was captured in the 1760s near the Slave Coast at age eleven and was first purchased by another African:

> At length, after many days' traveling, I got into the hands of a chieftain in a very pleasant country. This man had two wives and some children, and they all treated me extremely well and did all they could to comfort me, particularly the first wife, who was something like my mother. Although I was a great many days' journey from my father's house, yet these people spoke exactly the same language with us. This first master of mine, as I may call him, was a smith; and my principal employment

was working his bellows, which were the same kind as I had seen in my vicinity.

> . . . I was again sold. I was now carried to the left of the sun's rising, through many dreary wastes and dismal woods, amidst the hideous roarings of wild beasts. The people I was sold to used to carry me very often when I was tired, either on their shoulders or on their backs.[28]

In addition to the slave trade within Africa, the African east coast had been part of the Arab slave trade for centuries. Records show that black slaves were placed in Persian armies around A.D. 400—when Axum was thriving. In the tenth century Arab historian al-Masūdī wrote of his visit to Zanzibar. There he saw a vigorous trade in iron, ivory, tortoise-shell, cloth, and slaves. Perhaps one reason many Africans in East Africa readily accepted Islam in place of their traditional religion was survival. Islamic law forbade the enslavement of other Muslims.

Filled with Astonishment

Few documents survive to tell the slave trade story from the African slave's viewpoint. One of the most famous is The Early Travels of Olaudah Equiano, *written by Equiano in 1789. Captured at age eleven, Equiano was passed from one African owner to another and finally sold to British slave merchants. Equiano's book is included in* The African Past and the Coming of the Europeans, *edited by Leon Clark.*

"I had been about two or three days at the house of my new master when a wealthy widow, a neighbor of his, came there one evening and brought her only son, a young gentleman about my own age (11) and size. Here they saw me; and having taken a fancy to me, I was bought from the merchant, and went home with them. The next day I was washed and perfumed, and when mealtime came, I was led into the presence of my mistress and ate and drank before her with her son. This filled me with astonishment, and I could scarce help expressing my surprise that the young gentleman should suffer me, who was bound [a slave], to eat with him who was free; and not only so, but that he would not at any time either eat or drink till I had taken first, because I was the eldest, which was agreeable to our custom. Indeed, everything here, and all their treatment of me, made me forget that I was a slave.

The language of these people resembled ours so nearly that we understood each other perfectly. They had also the very same customs as we. There were likewise slaves daily to attend us, while my young master and I, with other boys, sported with our darts and bows and arrows, as I had been used to do at home."

African slaves of Arab masters were well treated, however, according to Islamic law. Slaves were often given responsible jobs and treated as members of the family, and intermarriage between Arab and African was very acceptable. In the Muslim world, slaves had rights and protection even though they were considered of the lowest class. Slaves could also regain their freedom.

To Europeans, however, a slave was simply a piece of property, not a human being with rights or protection. The owner had full power over that property. As early as 1441 twelve Africans from West Africa were carried to Portugal as captives. From then on, every Portuguese captain took slaves for his return voyage. By the mid-1400s coastal fishing villages were systematically raided by the Portuguese. Eventually the traders discovered it was easier to secure slaves by trading with Arab merchants of West Africa. They also developed networks with coastal African rulers, who sought a supply of captives from inland rulers. The following account of a Portuguese slave raid in 1446 is based on an early Portuguese document:

> "Let us return," said Antam Goncalvez, "to Cape Blanco, for I have heard that there is a village where we could find some people of whom we could make booty, if we took them suddenly and by surprise."
>
> Everyone agreed that this was a good idea and should be put into action at once. . . . The landing party moved on until they arrived at a certain high place, from which they could keep a good watch over all the parts around them. . . . So they captured in all fifty-five, whom they took with them to the boats. Of their joy I will not speak, because reason will tell you what it must have been, both of those who took the captives and of the others on board the ships, when they came with their prize.
>
> Wherefore they guided their ships toward Portugal, making straight for Lisbon, where they arrived quite content with their booty. . . . The next day . . . they took the captives out of the ships and conveyed them to the palace of the Prince. From all over the city, people flocked to the streets where they passed. Even those who had at first complained about such action [the bringing of captives from Africa] were now part of the cheering crowd.[29]

Some historians believe that their experience with African and Muslim ideas of slavery explains why African cultures participated so willingly in the European slave trade. Once captives were sold to European slavers, African rulers and merchants never saw the consequences of the sale.

European Notions of Africans

Since all of Africa was a great mystery to Europeans, it is not surprising that their notions of African people were often absurd. There were few writings available to add to those by Arab travelers to the merchant empires of the Sahel. European navigators were just beginning to write about contacts with coastal African people. Some accounts were accurate, but many were not. There was no way to know which accounts to believe, which descriptions were true. It was easy for European merchants and rulers to use the more absurd accounts to justify the slave trade. In the 1500s notions about Africans were influenced by Pliny's *A Summary of the Antiquities and Wonders of the World*. Pliny was a Roman who lived in the first century A.D. Where he got his ideas about Africa is a mystery. His account encouraged Europeans to see African people as animal-like subhumans. This attitude supported ideas about the slave trade.

> Of the Ethiopians [as all Africans were called] there are divers [various] forms and kinds of men. Some there are toward the east that have neither nose nor nostrils, but the face all full. Others that have no upper lip, they are without tongues, and they speak by signs, and they have but a little hole to take their breath at, by the which they drink with an oaten straw. There are

Both Europeans and Americans believed that the lives of captured African slaves would be improved once they were relocated to Christian countries.

some called Syrbote that are eight foot high, they live with . . . elephants. In a part of Affricke be people called Ptoemphane, for their king they have a dog, at whose fancy they are governed. . . . Toward the west there is a people called Arimaspi, that hath but one eye in their foreheads, they are in the desert and wild country. The people called Agriphagi live with the flesh of panthers and lions: and the people called Anthropomphagi which we call cannibals, live with human flesh. The Cinamolgi, their heads are almost like to the heads of dogs.[30]

There were other ideas that reinforced slavery. By capturing slaves, Europeans and Americans believed that the lives of Africans would actually be improved and that their souls would be rescued from heathenism by putting them in Christian countries. This was a widespread conviction in the American colonies, the destination for many of the West African slaves. American slave ship owners and captains were not low-life criminals or pirates. Instead, they were the most respected sea captains and merchants. They were leaders in their communities and active churchgoers. Slave buyers included the gentry of the south, like Thomas Jefferson, and Puritan ministers in New England.

It was the desire for profit that drove the European slave trade. Slaves were not valuable in Europe, where there was plenty of labor and no huge farming enterprises. In royal courts and noble homes, captive Africans became house servants. They were exhibited as a novelty, a prize, a sign of wealth. In the New World, it was a different story.

Only with the establishment of colonies in North and South America did large-scale slave trading become profitable—enormously profitable. In the colonies large farming and mining operations required great numbers of workers. At first the Spanish and Portuguese used the people of the West Indies as slaves. A gentle people, the Arawaks of the Caribbean islands soon died out from maltreatment as slaves and from despair. Who, then, would work the mines and the plantations?

The Spanish arranged for slaves through the Dutch, since the Spanish had no trade claims in West Africa. In the southern American colonies cheap, abundant labor was also desperately desired. Poor Englishmen agreed to become indentured servants and work for a number of years for low pay in the colonies until they finished their indentured time. However, there were not enough of them. The English began robbing Portuguese slave ships. Encouraged by Queen Elizabeth herself, English explorers like Sir Francis Drake began to develop their own slave trade. Eventually a private group calling themselves the Company of Royal Adventurers into Africa organized the slave trade for England.

Since the Portuguese were colonizing Brazil, it was not long before great numbers of slaves were being shipped there from the Congo coast. Once they established trade depots in the Congo-Angola area, suddenly the barren and unprofitable southwestern coast looked extremely valuable to the Portuguese. The Portuguese slave trade was ruthless and total in the area. No other area of Africa suffered as much from slavery as the population of Angola.

African Cooperation in the Slave Trade

The promise of big profits drew every European nation into the slave trade. It also drew many traditional African societies into the enterprise. Providing captives for slave merchants became the primary industry for many African kingdoms. For many coastal villagers, the choice was to be

The Brazilian slave trade (pictured) remained lucrative even after the country was colonized by Portugal. Numerous slaves were shipped to Brazil, greatly depleting the population of Angola.

enslaved themselves or to find others to take their place. By 1800 the heaviest slave trade occurred in a small strip of West African land called the Slave Coast, today's Togo, Dahomey, and part of Nigeria. The other area of heavy trading was Angola.

The profits of the slave trade were persuasive to African people. Europeans offered bars of iron, rolls of New World tobacco, lengths of linen, barrels of brandy, gold, and cowrie shells, which served as currency for some groups. And guns. The personal writings of a Dutch slave trader in the late 1600s show the importance of gun sales in the West African trade.

> Perhaps you wonder how the Negroes come to be furnished with firearms. But you will be astonished when you learn that we sell them incredible quantities. We are giving them the knife to cut our own throats. But we are forced to it, for if we did not, they might be supplied by the English, Danes or Brandenburghers [Germans]. And if we all agreed not to sell them any arms, the private traders would furnish them.
>
> Firearms and gunpowder have been the most popular merchandise here for a long time. If we did not supply them, we would not get our share of the trade.[31]

How Many Slaves?

It is almost impossible to find figures about the numbers of slaves sold out of Africa. So many countries were involved, and there are only fragments of informa-

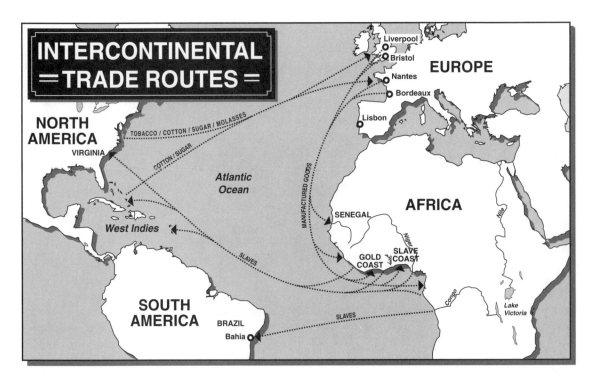

Delivering Slaves

Slaves living in Africa were servants with rights and protections. A letter from the early 1500s in Collins's African History *illustrates early African acceptance of European slavery.*

"Great caravans of negroes come here, bringing gold and slaves for sale. Some of the slaves have been captured in battle, others are sent by their parents, who think they are doing their children the best service in the world by sending them to be sold in this way to other lands where there is an abundance of provisions. They are brought as naked as they are born, both males and females, except for a sheepskin cloth; and they have glass rosaries [beads] of various colours, and articles made of glass, copper, brass and cotton cloths of different colours, and other similar things used throughout Ethiopia [Africa]."

tion available. Some of the information is unreliable because as the slave trade neared its end, nations and slave merchants looked for ways to disguise the true scope of the enterprise. They tried to put themselves in a more favorable light.

Some statistics are clear. During the 1500s the Spanish were rapidly developing mines and plantations in the New World. About four thousand African slaves a year were shipped to the Americas. That number increased to about seven thousand a year in the mid-1700s. At the same time, the Portuguese were shipping about ten thousand slaves a year to Brazil.

By 1800 the British had become the key players in the worldwide slave trade. The power and authority of the British fleet dominated the West African coast, except for the Congo-Angola area. In just nine years, records show, over ten thousand British ships had delivered over 356,000 slaves to the Americas—most to the United States. That was about 40,000 slaves a year.

Total figures of slaves sold throughout the years of the slave trade are only guesses. Most authorities agree that at least fifteen million Africans were sold. Many argue that the figures are at least double that, perhaps even triple. Millions more died in the packed middle passage decks of the slave ships. Most slavers lost one African in four during the middle passage; some lost one in three. Millions of Africans died in the raids for captives or on the forced march to the coast. Many died in the places where they were held before sailing. Olaudah Equiano wrote of his misery aboard a slave ship when he was twelve years old. His captivity under Europeans was a dramatic contrast to his captivity under Africans.

The blacks who brought me on board went off and left me abandoned to de-

Slaves were subjected to appalling conditions while crammed into middle passage decks of slave ships. An estimated one out of four slaves perished while in the overcrowded decks.

spair. . . . I even wished for my former slavery, in preference to my present situation, which was filled with horrors of every kind. . . . I was soon put down under the decks and there received such a smell in my nostrils as I had never experienced in my life; so that, with the horrible stench and crying together, I became so sick and low that I was not able to eat, nor had I the least desire to taste anything. I now wished for the last friend, death, to relieve me.

On my refusing to eat, one [white man] held me fast by the hands and laid me across a large bar and tied my feet while the other flogged me severely. I had never experienced anything of this kind before.[32]

Lasting Effects on Africa

How did this massive slave trade affect the development of Africa? Some areas, like Angola, experienced severe loss of population. As the demand for slaves grew, African rulers were often corrupted by greed for trade goods. As European weapons were accumulated through trade, war and violence were made easier. The kings invented wars and increased their slave raids. They used devious means to trick or capture men, women, and children for the slave merchants. Occasionally an African king would turn over his own people.

Religious life in African communities was sometimes misused to serve slavery, since rulers were religious leaders as well. For example, some rulers charged fines against those who offended the spirits. Offenders then had to either purchase or capture slaves to pay their fines. Tragically, traditional African arts and skills became devalued and even lost by some communities, since European products and styles took their place.

The usual trade patterns were changed and interrupted. Whole West African societies became totally dependent on the slave trade. The Slave Coast included today's Nigeria. Most slaves in the Niger River delta were purchased

African natives are yoked and deported by slave hunters. In some parts of Africa, native populations declined as the demand for slaves increased.

from inland groups. When asked how much he would lose if he gave up selling slaves, a Nigerian ruler answered, "If we cease to sell slaves to foreign ships, our principal source of wealth will be gone. The English were our first customers, and the trade has since been our chief means of support."[33]

Many of the rich and developing West African cultures were forcibly interrupted by the world slave trade, and their progress was permanently halted. African values became distorted. They were replaced by European ideas and methods of business and profit. A thirst for European trade goods and greed for easy wealth overran many African communities. Would four hundred years of slave trading ever end?

Protesting the Slave Trade

Although some African rulers fully cooperated in and profited from slave trading, others fought against it. One of the strongest fighters was Queen Nzinga of Angola, who became known as the queen who never surrendered. Queen Nzinga was both tough and smart. She protected escaped slaves and made frequent small-scale attacks against the Portuguese. For sixty years she led her army in the 1600s. A skillful negotiator, Nzinga made an alliance with the Dutch against the Portuguese. As Portuguese reinforcements were sent to Angola, Nzinga and her people retreated into the highlands and continued to fight from mountain strongholds.

Small groups of Americans and Europeans began to fight against slavery in the late 1600s. In the 1700s American Quakers, led by John Woolman, and some New England Puritan clergy began a campaign in the American colonies to end slavery. These leaders urged Americans to stop using crops like sugarcane, which were grown and harvested by slaves. Pressure in England, the greatest slave trading nation of all, came from the Society of Friends, or Quakers, and the Methodists under John and Charles Wesley. They viewed slavery as inhuman and evil, against the laws of God. By 1778, the Society for the Abolition of the Slave Trade was established in the American colonies and in England by 1787. Called abolitionists, most of the society members felt called by God to their work. They also felt a strong responsibility to slaves who had been freed, working to return them to Africa. In 1787, land was purchased in Sierra Leone by the British for the resettlement of freed slaves, and in 1847 Americans helped establish another independent homeland for freed slaves in West Africa, Liberia.

Conditions Worsen

Regardless of the efforts of the abolitionists, the momentum of the slave trade only increased. All aspects of American and English society were tied up in the slave trade. Too many people stood to lose too much. Even though a U.S. law was passed in 1820 making slave trading punishable by death, the slave trade was not affected. Enforcement was nonexistent, and the slave trade actually doubled after 1825.

Conditions for slaves became much worse. Specially designed slave ships crowded even more human cargo into smaller spaces. The food became worse, and no one was allowed on deck for fresh air or exercise. All this was to maintain secrecy and prevent detection as slavers, as the ships were called. In 1860 eighty-five new slave ships were outfitted in New York Harbor alone. In the last few months before the outbreak of the Civil War, fifteen thousand new slaves landed in the South.

New England citizens gather for an antislavery meeting. During the seventeenth and eighteenth centuries, many people began to call for the abolition of the slave trade.

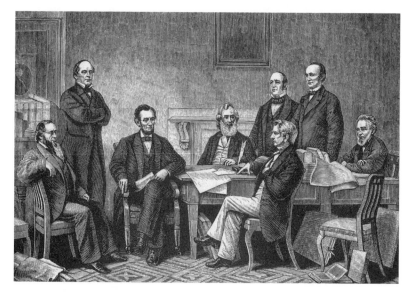

In 1863, President Abraham Lincoln signed the Emancipation Proclamation, a decree which abolished slavery in the United States.

The Ending of the Slave Trade

In the end, it took a combination of factors to close the door on the West African slave trade. Europeans and Americans became more and more convinced of the cruelty and immorality of slavery. They pressured their governments for firm action. Even though laws were passed abolishing every aspect of the slave trade, enforcement still remained a problem. In 1885 thirteen European countries and the United States pledged to stamp out the slave trade. They policed the seas and refused to supply guns or ammunition to violating nations.

In the heat of the campaign to eliminate slavery, abolitionists had some new ideas. If African people could support themselves in other ways, perhaps they would stop their activities in the slave trade. African rivers might serve as highways into the interior so that new trade routes could be opened. Then a variety of African products could support African cultures and replace the slave trade as their means of survival. This new trade would be a part of another effort: to bring Christianity into African life. Many Europeans felt reponsible for the evil of slavery. They hoped that new trade and Christianity would help undo that evil and improve their lives.

The strongest impact on slavery's end, however, was broad change in the world. Rapid industrialization was changing the world economy. The use of slaves became not only less necessary but less profitable. In the United States, slavery was finally abolished with the Emancipation Proclamation of 1863. It lingered on in Brazil, which was totally dependent on a slave-based economy, until 1885. Once the profit was gone, four hundred years of slavery finally came to an end.

The world's interest in Africa did not end, however. Opening the continent to science, industry, and Christianity became new goals in the mid-1800s.

7 Travelers' Tales, Explorers' Woes

Once the long coastline of Africa was opened to world trade, curiosity about Africa increased. What was the interior like beyond the coast? Much as the Europeans had feared the sea, they wondered: were there monsters and great evils deep inside Africa? Or were there amazing riches waiting to be found? With so many questions to answer, explorers left the comforts of home to search the unknown mysteries of Africa.

Curiosity About Africa

Scientists were fascinated with Africa. Everything about it intrigued them: its enormity, the promise of new plant and animal species, the mystery of its different climates. Above all, they were curious about its rivers and their origins. How could a mighty river like the Nile flow continually through a desert yet never run dry? The Nile became the frontier of scientific exploration.

To industrial leaders Africa appeared as a land of tremendous possibility. In the early 1800s many nations were building new business empires with modern machinery. Products could now be made faster, easier, and cheaper. To feed the new machines, however, factory owners needed raw materials, the ingredients to make the products. Finding cheap, plentiful raw materials was a big challenge. Industrialists thought that Africa might be a new source. The only way to know was to finance expeditions by explorers to learn everything possible about the mysterious African continent.

Of all the Europeans, the English were the most interested in opening Africa. English scientists were fascinated by the possibility of discovering and studying the geography and plant and animal life, along with the African peoples.

Several significant publications contributed to the drive toward exploration by providing remarkable descriptions of Africa and its people. Three former African slaves published their stories in the late 1700s, and these were widely read. One was Olaudah Equiano, who impressed European readers with his intelligence and writing skill. *Travels to Discover the Source of the Nile*, a book by a Scotsman, James Bruce, appeared around the same time. Dressed as a Muslim and posing as an Islamic scholar in Algeria and in Ethiopia, Bruce had spent about ten years in Africa. He discovered the source of the east branch of the Nile, the Blue Nile, in Ethiopia. The excitement in Europe over

While in Ethiopia, Scottish explorer James Bruce (right) discovered the source of the Blue Nile, a branch of the Nile River.

this find led to a new urgency to locate the ultimate source of the Nile.

As a result of these publications, Europeans arrived at some new conclusions. First, since African people were portrayed as human beings with interests and abilities similar to their own, Europeans reasoned that Africans were neither barbaric nor animal-like. Second, Europeans could travel in Africa in general safety and pursue significant scientific goals.

In 1788 an organization was created that reflected European fascination with Africa: the Association for Promoting Discovery of Interior Parts of Africa. It was better known as the Africa Association.

The Africa Association

Almost immediately the Africa Association began sponsoring expeditions into Africa. It was particularly interested in mapping the rivers, to see if they could be used to open inner Africa to trade. Scotsman Mungo Park made several journeys into West Africa for the Africa Association, and his reports were considered the greatest achievements of the association. Park reported that the Niger River flowed east, then south into the Atlantic. It did not flow west as had been imagined. His accounts also emphasized that while he had been treated cruelly by some African people, he was also compassionately treated by others. His experience with the Fulani people of West Africa provides a good example:

> I set off for the village, where I found, to my great mortification, that no person would admit me into his house. I was regarded with astonishment and fear, and was obliged to sit all day without victuals [food] in the shade of a tree; and the night threatened to be very uncomfortable, for the wind rose

Mungo Park, a Scottish explorer for the Africa Association, made several expeditions into West Africa and helped to expand knowledge of the Niger River.

and there was great appearance of a heavy rain. The wild beasts are so very numerous in the neighborhood, that I should have been under the necessity of climbing up the tree and resting amongst the branches.

About sunset . . . a woman, returning from the labours of the field, stopped to observe me, and perceiving that I was weary and dejected, inquired into my situation. Whereupon, with looks of great compassion . . . she told me to follow her. Having conducted me into her hut, she lighted a lamp, spread a mat on the floor, and told me I might remain there for the night. Finding that I was very hungry, she said she would procure me something to eat. She ac-cordingly went out and returned in a short time with a very fine fish . . . which she gave me for supper . . . the rites of hospitality being thus performed towards a stranger in distress.[34]

Reports like these heightened European interest in Africa. As one English leader announced, "We have already, by Mr. [Mungo] Park's means, opened a Gate into the Interior of Africa into which it is easy for every nation to enter and to extend its Commerce and Discovery from the West to the Eastern side of that immense continent."[35]

European countries accelerated their explorations of Africa in the mid-1800s. The greatest scientific prize of all was to discover the source of the Nile. Great

---

"Heaps of Broken Pedastals"

Scotsman James Bruce journeyed through northern Africa to the Sudan and Ethiopia, where he viewed the ruins of ancient Meroë. His description is included in The African Past, *a book of readings by Basil Davidson.*

"It was not till the eighth of May I had my audience of Sheikh Adelan at Aira, which is three miles and a half from Sennaar. We walked out early in the morning, for the greatest part of the way along the side of the Nile, which had no beauty, being totally divested of trees, the bottom foul and muddy. . . .

Beyond Shendi, about one hundred miles north of [Khartoum, on the Nile], we saw heaps of broken pedestals, like those of Axum, all plainly designed for the statues of the dog; some pieces of obelisk, likewise, with hieroglyphics, almost totally obliterated. The Arabs told us these ruins were very extensive, and that many pieces of statues, both of men and animals, had been dug up there. The statues of the men were mostly of black stone. It is impossible to avoid making a guess that this is the ancient city of Meroë."

While exploring Africa in 1863, Captain John Speke (far right) encountered many native groups and observed their traditional ceremonies.

Britain led the way with official, government-sponsored expeditions through the Royal Geographic Society. Other countries followed suit, creating their own geographic societies. Thus, new ventures into Africa had the full weight and authority of their governments behind them.

The great river Nile attracted a variety of adventurers. The spectacular journeys of Englishmen Richard Burton and John Speke reflected the times. Financed by the Royal Geographic Society, Burton and Speke made several journeys to find the so-called Mountains of the Moon, which were supposedly the origin of the Nile's waters. After enduring one crisis after another, the two men came to Lake Tanganyika, one of the Great Lakes of the Great Rift Valley.

Europeans adored the explorers. They loved hearing them describe animal attacks, death threats from African leaders, the horrors of malaria, and the drama of trekking through Africa. Traveling on his own in 1863, Speke was certain he had located the source of the Nile emerging from one of the Great Lakes. He named the huge lake Lake Victoria for the queen of England. But Burton was convinced the Nile flowed from Lake Tanganyika. Burton and Speke fought bitterly to get official endorsement of their separate claims, drawing even more public attention.

Just as interesting as Burton and Speke was the husband and wife team of big-game hunter Samuel Baker and his wife, Florence. In 1862 the Bakers worked their way along the upper reaches of the Nile while John Speke was busy on the same search. Separately from Speke, the Bakers also made their way to the Great Lakes. One of them they named Lake Albert, in honor of Queen Victoria's husband, Prince Albert. After this achievement the Bakers returned to southern Sudan and Uganda for four years. They were appointed to monitor the ongoing illegal slave trade and to put pressure on local leaders to end it.

David Livingstone

Even though Richard Burton, John Speke, and the Bakers all described the Great

The Royal Geographic Society commissioned David Livingstone, a doctor and Christian missionary, to verify the existence of the Great Lakes in Africa's interior.

Lakes in Africa's interior, European scientists wanted more proof of them. Did the large lakes really exist, and was one of them actually the source of the Nile? To settle this question, the Royal Geographic Society called on Dr. David Livingstone in 1865 to bring back a final answer.

A doctor and Christian missionary, David Livingstone began his work in Africa in 1840 at age twenty-three. Like others, he was convinced that introducing Christianity to Africa and opening Africa to the world would speed the end of the slave trade. However, Livingstone was as interested in the cultures and geography of Africa as in his missionary practice. He covered thousands of miles through central and southern Africa. He was the first white man seen by many Africans. A skilled writer, Livingstone wrote at length about African people and his observations:

The only avowed cause of dislike [of myself in one village] was expressed by a very influential and sensible man, the uncle of Sechele. "We like you as well as if you had been born among us. You are the only white man we can become familiar with. But we wish you to give up the everlasting preaching and praying. We can not become familiar with that at all. You see, we never get rain, while those tribes who never pray as we do obtain abundance." This was a fact, and we often saw it raining on the hills, ten miles off, while it would not look at us "even with one eye." If the Prince of the power of the air had no hand in scorching us, I fear I often gave him the credit for doing so.

As for the rain-makers, they carried the sympathies of the people along with them, and not without reason . . . and in order to understand their force we must place ourselves in their position, and believe, as they do, that all medicines act by a mysterious charm.[36]

By 1865 Livingstone had already crossed Africa from coast to coast through the jungle of the Congo basin. He had traversed the Kalahari Desert of today's Botswana. He was the first white person to see the great falls on the Zambezi River, which he named for Queen Victoria. All his books were widely read in Europe and the United States. It was not surprising, then, that the Royal Geographic Society chose Livingstone to verify the Great Lakes reports. When he accepted the mission, he wrote: "What my inclination leads me to prefer is to have intercourse with the people, and do what I can to enlighten them on the slave trade and give them some idea of our religion. . . . I shall enjoy myself, and feel that I am doing my duty."[37]

Henry Morton Stanley

In 1866 Livingstone set out on his Royal Geographic Society assignment. For three years there was no word from the famous man, and everyone feared the worst. Finally, a New York newspaper, the *Herald*, had a great publicity idea. It would send a reporter to find Dr. Livingstone. Young Henry Morton Stanley was given the assignment. In 1869 he organized a huge expedition to locate the missing explorer.

After eight months of tracing evidence of Livingstone in Africa, Stanley finally found him in 1871. Walking into the village of Ujiji, Tanzania, near Lake Tanganyika, Stanley found Livingstone in desperate circumstances. All his supplies and medicines were gone. The great man was sick and undernourished. In awe of this giant of African exploration, Stanley quietly greeted him with the now-famous words, "Dr. Livingstone, I presume?"

Stanley stayed with Livingstone for four months. With the doctor's letters and journals in hand, he returned to the United States. Livingstone continued his journey in Africa, but he never confirmed the source of the Nile. David Livingstone died in Africa in 1873 at age fifty-six. His faithful African companions had his body

In 1871, after months of trying to locate David Livingstone, Henry Morton Stanley finally found the explorer in Ujiji, Tanzania.

embalmed and carried it long and difficult miles to a seaport. When Livingtone's body arrived in England, it was for a hero's funeral. A newspaper account reported:

> Westminster Abbey had opened her doors to men who have played larger and greater parts in the history of mankind; but the feeling amongst many this afternoon was, that seldom has been admitted one more worthy—one more unselfish in his devotion to duty—one whose ruling desire was to benefit his kind and advance the sum of human knowledge and civilization—than the brave, modest, self-sacrificing African explorer.[38]

Henry Stanley went on to become a famous African explorer in his own right.

In the 1870s he confirmed the source of the Nile as Lake Victoria. He then traveled the full length of the treacherous waters of the Congo basin. In 1877 Stanley was near the end of his three-year journey across Africa. After surviving many battles with angry Africans and making it past the seven major waterfalls of the Congo River, Stanley wrote the following desperate letter:

> To any Gentleman who speaks English at Embomma [in Congo]
>
> Dear Sir,
>   I have arrived at this place from Zanzibar with 115 souls. . . . We are now in a state of imminent starvation. We can buy nothing from the natives, for they laugh at our kinds of cloth,

Fighting the Slave Trade

After his first exploration in Africa, Samuel Baker was sent back by the British government to the Sudan. His assignment was to help stop the slave trade still flourishing there. This excerpt of Samuel Baker's 1879 book about the upper Nile region, is excerpted in African History, *by Robert Collins.*

"Upon existing conditions the Soudan is worthless, having neither natural capabilities nor political importance. But there is, nevertheless, a reason that first prompted its occupation by the Egyptians, and that is in force to the present day (1870). The Soudan supplies slaves.

Without the White Nile trade, Khartoum would almost cease to exist; and that trade is kidnapping and murder. . . . The people for the most part engaged in the nefarious [vicious] traffic of the White Nile are Syrians, Copts, Turks, Circassians and some few Europeans. . . . Every one in Khartoum, with the exception of a few Europeans, was in favour of the slave-trade and looked with jealous eyes upon a stranger venturing within the precincts of their holy land. A land sacred to slavery and to every abomination and villainy that man can commit."

beads, and wire. . . . I am told there is an Englishman at Embomma, and as you are a Christian and a gentleman, I beg you not to disregard my request. . . . [I want] fifteen man-loads of rice or grain to fill their pinched bellies immediately. . . . The supplies must arrive within two days, or I may have a fearful time of it among the dying. . . .

Yours sincerely,

H. M. Stanley

Commanding Anglo-American Expedition for Exploration of Africa

P.S. You may not know my name; therefore I add, I am the person that discovered Livingstone in 1871. H.M.S.[39]

A relief party was sent immediately, and Stanley reached the Atlantic eight days after his letter. Stanley returned to Africa several times. He was convinced that the world would profit from the natural riches he had seen throughout his travels.

A reputed African explorer, Henry Stanley confirmed the source of the Nile River and explored the waters of the Congo basin.

The Effects of Explorations

When David Livingstone first walked into Africa in 1841, Europeans had primarily contacted only the edges of the continent. In thirty years major changes occurred. Early explorers became heroes to Europeans and were viewed as experts on Africa. Sometimes they exaggerated the details about the continent to impress the world. Industrialists became persuaded that no risks were too great to claim Africa's natural riches. Christian groups began to compete for influence in Africa. While many missionary groups respected African life and traditions, some did not. In their rush to bring European civilization to African people, missionaries often disregarded African values and traditions.

By 1870 Africa's door had been pried wide open. African societies would not be isolated much longer, and soon their traditional ways of life would be seriously threatened.

8 Carving Up Africa

By 1870 Africa was no longer the great mystery it once was. As trade between Africa and the rest of the world increased, changes in the continent accelerated. Africa's natural wealth poured out through foreign railroads and foreign ships. People of the traditional cultures found themselves second-class citizens, without value and influence.

Competition over Africa

The rapid industrialization of Europe and North America created a strong demand for African raw materials. As new trade commodities, Africa's oil, iron ore, and other minerals were very valuable. Markets for palm oil and rubber were quickly developed. A base for soaps and lotions, palm oil was also useful in industry as a lubricant. Before the invention of the automobile, rubber was already in great demand for factory belts, buggy tires, and many industrial uses.

The seaports and elaborate trade routes developed for the slave trade were now used to ship both old and new products. Luxury items like gold and ivory had always been major trade items. Modern nations prized ivory for piano keys, knife

A British freighter docks at a crowded African port. Competition over Africa's natural riches increased as industrialization swept across Europe and North America.

African ivory is accumulated at a campsite in the Congo basin. Modern nations turned the ivory trade into a major business, using ivory to create luxury items ranging from piano keys to jewelry.

handles, carved art, and jewelry. Once diamonds and new gold sources were discovered in South Africa, they became a major source of wealth for the British. It was not long before nations competed over African products. Who would have control over each trade area, each seaport?

Who Controls Africa?

By 1880 many European countries had occupied, purchased, or seized parts of Africa. Through force and determination, foreign officials kept extending their control over more and more African people. Each country claimed the right to control portions of Africa. Africa's natural wealth promised great profits, so the stakes were high.

Great Britain, France, and Portugal had long been active in Africa. They had firmly claimed exclusive trading rights in certain areas that they called their territories. The French controlled most of West

Africa. The Portuguese dominated the Congo-Angola coast. The British claimed South Africa, the Slave Coast, and Gold Coast, from Nigeria to Ghana.

Strong rivalries in Europe affected these claims. The countries that felt left out asserted their rights to establish colonies in Africa as well. Some of these countries, like Germany, had become powerful in Europe. The potential benefits of cheap raw materials and easy profits were very attractive. Some nations began to assert dubious claims to certain areas in Africa and to threaten the boundaries of neighboring territories. Threats between old and new rivals over African claims worried world leaders, for war seemed likely if conflicts over territory could not be resolved.

To prevent the outbreak of war over African territory, the Berlin Conference of 1884–1885 set up some rules. Twelve European nations, Turkey, and the United States attended the conference. It did not occur to these nations to invite African leaders to the conference. The fourteen nations attending all came to agreement: no country could claim control or primary influence over an area unless it effectively *occupied and governed the area.* This meant that sweeping claims by explorers or traders meant nothing. It was up to the sponsoring countries to create a permanent, governing presence in the area. Otherwise, there were no legal claims to the territory and no boundary lines could be recognized.

Effects of the Berlin Conference

The race to conquer all of Africa began the day the Berlin Conference ended. Several countries had head starts, but many others now seriously joined the competition. Foreign countries rushed to claim land and begin to govern the Africans under their control. Europeans could create boundaries that divided kingdoms in half or separated ancient family groups from one another. All the old language and kinship bonds were threatened as European leaders drew lines on maps or put stakes in the ground. The new lines and new boundaries had nothing to do with African history or tradition, only with claims to territory and control for outsiders.

Impatient to speed the division of Africa, European nations used force and coercion to bring African people under control. Treaties were often made with African rulers. If there was resistance, there was no reluctance by Europeans to force an agreement. With strength of weapons and a drive toward domination, the European countries pushed inland as quickly as possible. They annexed village after village, mile after mile. Germans, Italians, and Belgians joined the Dutch, French, British, and Portuguese until the African continent was completely carved up into their own colonies.

Subjugation of Africa

The thirty years between 1880 and 1910 were years of misery for Africa. Brutal treatment of Africans, as horrible as during the years of the slave trade, was common during these years. The worst abuses of all were in the Congo. Explorer Henry Stanley opened the Congo basin and hoped the British would be interested in the natural riches of the territory. When the British did not respond, King Leopold of Belgium approached Stanley.

In spite of claims made by other nations, Stanley arranged for King Leopold to control the Congo by negotiating land concessions from Congolese chiefs. The Berlin Conference reluctantly accepted Leopold's claim to the Congo Free State, which included the mouth of the Congo River. King Leopold then proceeded to cruelly control the Congolese people. They were forced to work for Belgian overseers and deprived of food, family, and familiar surroundings. In spite of their active and ongoing resistance, large numbers of Congolese people were moved about at gunpoint to labor wherever needed for Leopold's ventures.

King Leopold's policies were hidden to the world until around 1900, when evidence of Belgian brutalities was made known. Enforced servitude, arbitrary shootings, and starvation of huge numbers of Congolese people over twenty years had destroyed the Congo basin population. It had been reduced from over twenty million people to eight million. But King Leopold had become a very rich man.

African Resistance

How did African societies react to the takeover of their homelands? Resistance was vigorous and widespread as early as the 1600s by leaders like Queen Nzinga. In 1890 the people of Tanganyika, today's

After gaining control of the Congo Free State, King Leopold of Belgium brutally forced the Congolese people into servitude and deprived them of food, family, and familiar surroundings.

Tanzania, rose against the Germans in the Maji-Maji rebellion. As one of the last countries to seek a foothold in Africa, Germany rushed to create German East Africa. The Germans burned villages and cruelly attacked the African rebels with overwhelming force. Over one hundred thousand Africans died in Tanganyika.

During the creation of German West Africa, today's Namibia, the Herero people rebelled in 1903 against forced labor and loss of their communities. By the time the rebellion was crushed by the Germans, two-thirds of the Herero had died.

The following letter reveals the courage demonstrated by African leaders as they faced the power of their colonizers. It was written by Tanganyika's Chief Macemba in 1890 to the Germans he was fighting:

I have listened to your words but can find no reason why I should obey you—I would rather die first. I have no relations with you and can not bring it to my mind that you have given me so much as . . . a needle or a thread. I look for some reason why I should obey you and find not the smallest. If it should be friendship that you desire, then I am ready for it, today and always; but to be your subject, that I can not be. If it should be war you desire, then I am ready, but never to be your subject. . . . I do not fall at your feet, for you are God's creature just as I am. . . . I am sultan here in my land. You are sultan there in yours. Yet listen, I do not say to you that you should obey me; for I know that you [are] a free man. As for me, I will not come to you, and if you are strong enough, then come and fetch me.[40]

The powerful Zulu leader Shaka (left) ruled a large region of South Africa during the 1800s. Feared by both the Dutch and British, Shaka and his forces created strong opposition to colonization.

In the early 1800s in South Africa, a strong Zulu leader named Shaka dominated a large region of the colony. In twelve years Shaka conquered smaller groups of South Africans and united them with the Zulu people into a territory larger than France. He gave them a sense of uniform social structure, power, and dignity in the face of colonial forces. Shaka was feared by the Dutch and the British. Although often cruel and ruthless even to African people under his control, Shaka created a powerful opposition force to colonization. His highly trained armies were surprisingly effective, even though they lacked modern weapons. A British soldier in South Africa described a Zulu warrior's military equipment and supplies:

A warrior's war outfit consisted of a shield made out of dried ox-hide, oval in shape, about 2 feet 6 inches wide and long enough for the owner to look over. . . . His offensive arms consisted of from two to three assagais [spears], one of which would be the stabbing assagai . . . that had a blade of at least a foot to 18 inches long fixed to a strong shaft of wood about 2 feet in length. . . . The Zulu warrior was not encouraged to throw his assagai but was taught to rush in, defend himself with his shield and stab home with

In the late 1800s in Kenya, the British decided to subjugate the Kikuyu people through ruthless pacification expeditions. Captain Meinertzhagen of the King's African Rifles recorded this passage in his journal. It is included in East Africa, *edited by Cottrell and Gaisford.*

"I have performed a most unpleasant duty today. . . . [In response to the murder of a white man] I gave orders that every living thing except children be killed without mercy. Every soul was either shot or bayoneted. . . . We systematically cleared the valley in which the village was situated, burnt all huts, and killed a few more niggers. . . .

The Kikuyu are ripe for trouble, and when they get educated and medicine men are replaced by political agitators there will be a general rising. . . . I cannot see millions of educated Africans—as there will be in a hundred years' time—submitting tamely to white domination. After all, it is an African country, and they will demand domination. Then blood will be spilled, and I have little doubt about the eventual outcome."

[it]. He also carried a knobkerry [club] and a plain stick both made of hard wood. His food, carried for him by a boy, consisted of a small bag of dried meat and grain.[41]

The most successful African leader to resist foreign conquest of his territory was Emperor Menelik II of Ethiopia. In the 1880s Italy, having no claims to African territory, desperately tried to squeeze into Africa. The area selected by Italy was the Somali coast and eventually Ethiopia. Once its flag was planted on the Somali shore, Italy declared it would soon control nearby Ethiopia. Menelik was outraged. He announced to all of Europe that he had no intention of allowing Italian control over his country.

While tracing today the actual boundaries of my Empire, I shall endeavour,

Emperor Menelik II of Ethiopia resisted the partitioning of Africa by foreign countries. In 1896, Menelik and his troops crushed the Italian army as it sought to conquer Ethiopia and the Somali coast.

if God gives me life and strength, to reestablish the ancient frontiers of Ethiopia up to Khartoum, and as far as Lake Nyanza, with all the Gallas. Ethiopia has been for 14 centuries a Christian island in a sea of pagans. If powers at a distance come forward to partition Africa between them, I do not intend to be an indifferent spectator![42]

Menelik prepared for war. When the Italian and Ethiopian armies met in 1896, the Italians were soundly defeated. Menelik had proved that a European nation could be defeated by Africans. He remained a hero to all Africans until his death in 1913.

Although African people all over the continent had used fierce resistance and great endurance, they were overwhelmed by the colonial powers. European weapons controlled the relationships. Even though many Africans had accumulated stockpiles of weapons, newer and larger numbers of efficient weapons, such as early machine guns, were always in the hands of the Europeans.

French and British Plans

As foreign countries moved toward total control of Africa, both the French and British had grand schemes. The French moved swiftly to extend their influence in western Africa. With the exception of a few small areas, they had soon created French West Africa. It was a huge area stretching from the Mediterranean Sea down to Cameroon—the entire hump of Africa.

Cecil Rhodes, prime minister of South Africa in the 1890s, believed that the British should control all of East Africa. He worked toward developing a solid corridor of British power from Egypt to South Africa. By 1910 Great Britain had established colonies in Egypt, Sudan, Uganda, Kenya, Zimbabwe, Botswana, and South Africa. Rhodes's goal was almost a reality.

Like many Europeans, Rhodes was convinced that Africans were an inferior race, and because of this, that Europeans had the right to control the destiny of Africa. These attitudes supported European self-interest. Although Europeans no longer believed that Africans were strange, and nonhuman, they still believed that African people were uncivilized, back-

During his reign as prime minister of South Africa, Cecil Rhodes helped to secure British control over eastern Africa.

ward, and people of little intelligence with inferior culture. Europeans were convinced that it was the destiny of non-Africans to bring Africa into prosperity and the world arena. This attitude was expressed by Ewart Grogan, an Englishman who settled in the British colony of Kenya:

> A good sound system of compulsory labor would do more to raise the nigger in five years than all the millions that had been sunk in missionary efforts for the past fifty. . . . Let the native be compelled to work for many months in the year at a fixed and reasonable rate and call it compulsory education. . . . Under such a title, surely the most delicate British conscience may be at rest.[43]

Dismantling Africa

In 1880 over 90 percent of Africa was controlled by African people. By 1900 only Liberia and Ethiopia remained under African rule. The independent societies of Africa had been dismantled and the vitality of their cultures destroyed.

While the uniqueness of many African cultures was being destroyed, remnants were saved. Wherever possible, African groups and individuals struggled to preserve their heritage and to pass it on to their children. Centuries of African independence and cultural development were over, but the contributions of those years would not die.

Traditional Africa Endures

Colonial rule was never accepted by most Africans. Forms of African resistance continued from the 1880s through World War II. After World War II the desire to be free of foreign domination became a powerful force. One by one, African countries gradually became independent. Some suffered through long years of war and hardship. Today each African country looks to its ancient heritage for strength and inspiration. Some countries reclaimed their ancient names: Mali, Namibia, Ghana,

In modern Africa, ancient cultures and traditions continue to exist in a twentieth-century world.

Zimbabwe. African museums honor ancient cultures. Traditional principles and religion exist alongside twentieth-century ideas and religious groups.

Africa's Legacy

The contributions to world civilization from the African cultures are increasingly understood and appreciated by the wider world. African kingdoms and societies created notable achievements in government, literature, architecture, economics, religion, and the arts. The strength of the African peoples enabled them to adapt to change and to survive. Sometimes they were challenged by dramatic changes in climate, at other times by foreign invaders of their land. Certain strong African principles remain to this day: valuing the benefits to the group over the individual; the integration of the spirit world into daily life; and vibrant creativity in art and music. These are just some of the ways in which Africa continues to make unique contributions to world civilization.

Notes

Chapter 1: Birthplace of Humanity

1. Richard E. Leakey, *The Making of Mankind.* New York: E. P. Dutton, 1981.
2. Mina White Mulvey, *Digging up Adam: The Story of L. S. B. Leakey.* New York: David McKay Company, 1969.
3. Mulvey, *Digging up Adam.*
4. Peter Garlake, *The Kingdoms of Africa.* New York: Peter Bedrick Books, 1990.

Chapter 2: Great Empires in West Africa

5. Garlake, *The Kingdoms of Africa.*
6. Quoted in Basil Davidson, *African Kingdoms.* New York: Time, Inc., 1966.
7. Quoted in Alvin M. Josephy Jr., ed., *The Horizon History of Africa.* New York: American Heritage, 1971.
8. Quoted in Josephy, *The Horizon History of Africa.*
9. Quoted in Robert O. Collins, ed., *African History: Text and Readings.* New York: Random House, 1971.
10. Quoted in Josephy, *The Horizon History of Africa.*
11. Quoted in Collins, *African History.*
12. Quoted in Collins, *African History.*

Chapter 3: The Glories of East Africa

13. Quoted in Josephy, *The Horizon History of Africa.*
14. Quoted in Josephy, *The Horizon History of Africa.*
15. Quoted in Josephy, *The Horizon History of Africa.*
16. Garlake, *The Kingdoms of Africa.*
17. Quoted in Josephy, *The Horizon History of Africa.*
18. Garlake, *The Kingdoms of Africa.*

Chapter 4: Tradition in Central and Southern Africa

19. Quoted in Collins, *African History.*
20. Quoted in Josephy, *The Horizon History of Africa.*
21. Tepilit Ole Saitoti, *The Worlds of a Maasai Warrior.* Berkeley: University of California Press, 1986.
22. Quoted in Basil Davidson, *The African Past.* Boston: Little, Brown, 1964.

Chapter 5: Sailing for Riches

23. Quoted in Davidson, *The African Past.*
24. Quoted in Eldred D. Jones, *The Elizabethan Image of Africa.* Washington, DC: Folger Shakespeare Library, 1971.
25. Quoted in Robert Coughlan and the *Life* editors, *Tropical Africa.* New York: Time, Inc., 1962.
26. Quoted in Davidson, *African Kingdoms.*
27. Quoted in E. Jefferson Murphy, *The History of African Civilization.* New York: Dell Publishing, 1974.

Chapter 6: The Impact of the Slave Trade

28. Quoted in Leon Clark, ed., *The African Past and the Coming of the Europeans.* New York: Praeger, 1970.
29. Quoted in Clark, *The African Past and the Coming of the Europeans.*
30. Quoted in Jones, *The Elizabethan Image of Africa.*
31. Quoted in Clark, *The African Past and the Coming of the Europeans.*
32. Quoted in Clark, *The African Past and the Coming of the Europeans.*

33. Quoted in Leon Clark, *The African Past and the Coming of the Europeans.*

Chapter 7: Travelers' Tales, Explorers' Woes

34. Quoted in Collins, *African History.*

35. Quoted in Susan Clinton, *The World's Great Explorers: David Livingstone and Henry Morton Stanley.* Chicago: Childrens Press, 1990.

36. Quoted in Murphy, *The History of African Civilization.*

37. Quoted in Murphy, *The History of African Civilization.*

38. Quoted in Clinton, *The World's Great Explorers.*

39. Quoted in Thomas Sterling, *Exploration of Africa.* New York: American Heritage, 1963.

Chapter 8: Carving Up Africa

40. Quoted in Murphy, *The History of African Civilization.*

41. Quoted in Josephy, *The Horizon History of Africa.*

42. Quoted in Murphy, *The History of African Civilization.*

43. Quoted in John Cottrell and John Gaisford, eds., *East Africa.* Alexandria, VA: Time-Life Books, 1987.

Glossary

A.D.: Referring to historical dates after the year of the birth of Jesus Christ, which is considered year 1; European, or Western world history uses the Christian calendar as its base.

age of metals: The period in human history when knowledge of working copper, bronze, and iron was available, beginning around 600 B.C. in Africa.

anthropologist: One who studies the origin, culture, and development of human beings.

archaeologist: A person who studies the history of people and their cultures through their artifacts.

barter: To exchange goods instead of using a form of currency for payment.

B.C.: Referring to historical dates before the year of the birth of Jesus Christ.

cataract: Rapids or waterfalls.

coercion: The use of force to achieve agreement.

fossil: The remains or trace of a living thing, usually in rock, from a previous geological age.

hieroglyphics: A form of writing using pictures or symbols.

hominid: An anthropological term referring to human or humanlike species.

mosque: Building used as center of Islamic study and prayer.

nomad: A person who moves frequently and does not live in a permanent site.

plateau: A geological formation of elevated but level land.

Sahel: The semi-arid region immediately to the south of the Sahara Desert.

savanna: A grassland plain with scattered trees that receives occasional rainfall, usually twice a year.

stelae: Tall stone monuments, frequently covered with carved symbols and decorations.

Stone Age: The period in human history when stone tools alone were used, beginning around 2.4 million years B.C. in Africa.

strategic: Of key importance.

terra-cotta: A brownish-orange clay often used for sculpture. When fired and glazed for housewares, it is also called earthenware.

tributaries: Secondary streams that flow into the primary river or stream.

wadi: A seasonal riverbed that runs with water only during a rainy season.

For Further Reading

Susan Clinton, *The World's Great Explorers: David Livingstone and Henry Morton Stanley.* Chicago: Childrens Press, 1990. This very attractive book features many black-and-white and color photographs, historical illustrations, and African landscapes. Using simple, clear language, it reads like an action-packed novel. It also provides a balanced treatment of the effects of exploration on Africa. The book includes a timeline, glossary, index, and vintage map of exploration journeys.

Maitland Edey and the editors of Time-Life Books, *The Missing Link: The Emergence of Man.* New York: Time-Life Books, 1972. *The Missing Link* has good illustrations related to early humans in an African setting and an excellent section with illustrations on weapons and tools. The text is now dated in places, but it is worth consulting. It has interesting charts and diagrams and a bibliography. While the text may be too difficult for some readers, the illustrations are valuable.

Lawrence Fellows, *East Africa.* New York: Macmillan, 1972. This is a valuable volume because it unites the histories of the major countries of East Africa: Uganda, Kenya, and Tanzania, helping readers see the artificiality of today's modern national boundaries stemming from colonialism. The first fifty pages focus on the geography of the region and early history through colonialism. There are black-and-white photographs, a good reading list, and an index.

John A. J. Gowlett, *Ascent to Civilization: The Archaeology of Early Man.* New York: Alfred A. Knopf, 1984. This is an excellent introduction to current understanding of humankind's origins, with strong sections on Africa. Large, colorful illustrations include outstanding three-dimensional maps, site reconstructions, charts, and photographs. While the text may be a bit dense, parts of it are quite suitable for student use. Available in paperback.

Edwin P. Hoyt, *African Slavery.* New York: Ablard-Achuman Ltd., 1973. This readable volume contains excellent stories about individuals, including slaves, reformers, traders, and others. It provides important and balanced perspectives on the slave trade, including recent information. It is one of the finest resources on this subject. The illustrations are black and white with many original woodcuts and engravings.

Constance Jones, *Africa 1500–1900.* New York: Facts On File, 1993. This is a valuable history with denser text than most young people's books. There are good maps, a few black-and-white illustrations, a chronology, an index, and a bibliography.

Jane Kerina, *African Crafts.* New York: Lion Press, 1970. This is an excellent volume for middle-grade students. It includes brief descriptions of African crafts with accompanying illustrations. Best of all, many of the crafts have been adapted so that young people can make versions of the crafts themselves.

Jason Laure, *Namibia.* Chicago: Childrens Press, 1993. Part of the Enchantment of the World series, *Namibia* features many black-and-white and color photographs and excellent maps. It includes one-page summaries on subjects like geography, the economy, important people, and holidays. The first three chapters focus on the natural environment, early history, and the colonial period. This huge series includes fifteen books on Africa, ten of which cover the area south of the Sahara.

Jocelyn Murray, *Africa: A Cultural Atlas for Young People.* New York: Facts On File, 1990. A beautifully illustrated book with many excellent maps. The text is organized into compact two-page themes and topics. A large-format hardcover book, it covers both ancient and modern African history.

Sean Sheehan, *Zimbabwe.* New York: Marshall Cavendish Corporation, 1993. Beautifully illustrated with many color photographs, this readable volume is part of the Cultures of the World series. There are chapters on geography, early history such as of Great Zimbabwe, religion, language, ethnic groups, and many other topics. It is well organized and appealing in its overall design. Other books on Africa in the series include *Kenya, Nigeria, South Africa,* and *Libya.* The book includes a map, index, glossary, and bibliography.

Al Stark, *Zimbabwe: A Treasure of Africa.* Minneapolis: Dillon Press, 1986. A Discover Our Heritage book, *Zimbabwe* is especially good for students with simpler language skills. Good content is interspersed with humor, down-to-earth examples, and stories. There is an excellent summary of the early history. The book includes a glossary with pronunciation guide, a bibliography, and an index.

David Sweetman, *Woman Leaders in African History.* Portsmouth, NH: Heinemann Educational Books, 1984. Part of a series, African History Biographies, this is a valuable and fascinating book covering twelve significant women leaders from ancient times to the 1890s. Illustrations are small and only in black and white, but the text is insightful, and inspiring. Each chapter provides a reading list. For advanced readers. Available in paperback.

John Waechter, *Man Before History*, rev. ed. New York: Peter Bedrick Books, 1990. A volume in The Making of the Past series. Chapter 4 is about the beginnings of humankind in Africa; other parts of the book illuminate the development of humankind worldwide. Appropriate for advanced readers, *Man Before History* is valuable for any age level because of its excellent illustrations, thorough and partially illustrated glossary, bibliography, and index. Available in paperback.

David Wisniewski, *Sundiata: Lion King of Mali.* New York: Clarion Books, 1992. This is a spectacularly illustrated picture book with accurate details and excellent text. It introduces important terminology, geographic locations, and the power of the historical figure of Sundiata. There is an excellent historical summary page at the end of the volume. Appealing to all reading and age levels.

Works Consulted

Leon Clark, ed., *The African Past and the Coming of the Europeans.* New York: Praeger, 1970. This is the third unit of *Through African Eyes: Cultures in Change.* It is a valuable book of readings that include excerpts from African writers, historians, political figures, and historical documents.

Robert O. Collins, ed., *African History: Text and Readings.* New York: Random House, 1971. This volume is packed with excellent readings from primary sources related to each major region south of the Sahara, ranging from the writings of Ibn Battutah in the 1300s to Nelson Mandela's writings in the 1950s. Each section of writings is preceded by a brief historic summary of the region.

John Cottrell and John Gaisford, eds., *East Africa.* Alexandria, VA: Time-Life Books, 1987. Part of the Library of Nations series, *East Africa* has a helpful chronology and some well-designed maps. Half the volume is devoted to the postcolonial development of East Africa, with good historical material and commentary on modern East Africa.

Basil Davidson, *Africa in History*, rev. ed. New York: Collier Books, 1991. As the author of over twenty books on Africa, Basil Davidson is recognized as a balanced authority with deep respect for African history and cultures. This is a solid, readable volume with a good annotated bibliography and chronology. Available in paperback.

——, *African Kingdoms.* New York: Time, Inc., 1966. A volume in the series, Great Ages of Man: A History of the World's Cultures, it is magnificently illustrated with excellent maps, including a relief map of the continent. There are helpful reconstruction drawings of early cities and cultures and a time line chart comparing the changes in civilizations throughout African history. Advanced young readers would enjoy this book.

——, *The African Past.* Boston: Little, Brown, 1964. In this volume Davidson has collected a series of readings from primary sources, ranging from the earliest recorded observations of Africa to the 1960s.

Peter Garlake, *The Kingdoms of Africa.* New York: Peter Bedrick Books, 1990. A volume in the series, Making of the Past, it emphasizes the impact of archaeology and related specific disciplines on our understanding of history. It is well organized with excellent photographs and a unique illustrated glossary. While oriented to adults, the book is valuable for advanced young readers. Available in paperback.

Alvin M. Josephy Jr., ed., *The Horizon History of Africa.* New York: American Heritage, 1971. A hefty volume packed with rich illustrations, charts, and maps, this book has numerous primary documents included in the text ranging from Yoruba songs and riddles to writings of Islamic scholars.

Richard E. Leakey, *The Making of Mankind.* New York: E. P. Dutton, 1981. Archaeologist and anthropologist Richard Leakey has written a thorough summary of the exploration for human ancestors up to 1981. It includes frequent commentary on possible applications of new information to our understanding of modern human behavior. With large artists' impressions of early human life, color photographs, and maps, the book was designed to accompany a television series of the same name. It also reflects Leakey's personal style of reflection and humor.

Roger Lewin, *In the Age of Mankind: A Smithsonian Book of Human Evolution.* Washington, DC: Smithsonian Books, 1988. This beautifully illustrated book has strong material on African archaeology, with interesting sections on the Leakey family and Richard Leakey's recent work, as well as other leading African archaeologists like Donald Johanson, the discoverer of Lucy.

G. Mokhtar, ed., *Ancient Civilizations of Africa: General History of Africa II.* Berkeley: University of California Press, 1981. This is part of an important eight-volume series resulting from UNESCO's International Scientific Commission for the Drafting of a General History of Africa. The chapters are dense with information written by world experts, whose brief biographies are included. There is a brief helpful conclusion.

E. Jefferson Murphy, *The History of African Civilization.* New York: Dell Publishing, 1974. This is one of the most insightful, thorough, and readable histories on Africa. It provides excellent balance and perspective.

Thomas Sterling, *Exploration of Africa.* New York: American Heritage, 1963. A volume in the Horizon Caravel Series, this book traces the dramatic experiences of European explorers in search of adventure.

John Thornton, *Africa and Africans: In the Formation of the Atlantic World, 1400–1680.* New York: Cambridge University Press, 1992. A volume in the Studies of Comparative World History series. This is an in-depth discussion of the complexity of the slave trade and its impact on the development of the New World. Available in paperback.

Index

Picture Credits

Cover photo: North Wind Picture
   Archives
Archive Photos, 58, 73, 77, 80, 82
The Bettmann Archive, 16, 45, 55, 63, 70,
   71
Culver Pictures, Inc., 39, 49, 52, 67
   (bottom), 78, 79
Hulton Deutsch Collection Limited, 37,
   67 (top), 69

Erich Lessing/Art Resource, 17
Library of Congress, 46, 50, 64
North Wind Picture Archives, 10, 22, 25,
   36, 47, 53, 54, 65, 74, 75
Blair Seitz/Art Resource, 34
Stock Montage, Inc., 31
UPI/Bettmann, 12, 13, 15, 41
Werner Forman Archive/Art Resource,
   19, 20, 30, 40

About the Author

Artist and historian Louise Minks has a master's degree in American history and teaches part time at Greenfield Community College in Greenfield, Massachusetts. She created a touring art exhibition on Kenya and has written and illustrated a limited-edition handmade book called *African Album.* She has coauthored with her husband two young adult books, *The French and Indian War* and *The American Revolution.* Minks has also written an art book called the *The Hudson River School.*

Minks and her husband live in Leverett, Massachusetts, with their two daughters.